I0422254

Contents

Preface: 3

Expanded Table of Contents...7

Chapter 1. Introduction to Machine Learning 10

Chapter 2. Python Basics...12

Chapter 3. Libraries and Frameworks 16

Chapter 4. Data Preprocessing..19

Chapter 5. Exploratory Data Analysis (EDA): Descriptive Statistics 32

Chapter 6. Supervised Learning: Regression and Classification Algorithms
....44

Chapter 7. Unsupervised Learning: Clustering Algorithms 57

Chapter 8. Ensemble Learning: Bagging and Boosting Techniques 66

Chapter 9. Neural Networks and Deep Learning: Introduction to Neural
Networks..74

Chapter 10. Natural Language Processing (NLP) 85

Chapter 11. Model Deployment 100

Chapter 12. Reinforcement Learning 112

Chapter 13. Model Interpretability 126

Chapter 14. Advanced Topics...139

Chapter 15. Case Studies 159

Chapter 16. Ethical Considerations 172

Chapter 17. Future Trends 176

Chapter 18. Hands-On Projects 182

Chapter 19: Advanced Data Visualization Techniques 185

Chapter 20: Time Series Analysis 208

Chapter 21: Recommender Systems...231

Chapter 22: Anomaly Detection 245

Appendix...263

Sample Solutions to End of Chapter Problems.........................277

Preface:

Welcome to the world of Python Machine Learning Essentials! In this book, authored by Bernard Baah, CEO of Filly Coder (https://fillycoder.com) and an experienced educator with six years of teaching Python and a dozen other programming languages, we embark on an exciting journey through the realms of artificial intelligence and data-driven decision-making. Bernard, who has also authored books on Python Fundamentals, Python Data Analysis, the use of AI in Software Development, and web development, brings a wealth of knowledge and expertise to this comprehensive guide.

About This Book:

Title: Python Machine Learning Essentials

Author: Bernard Baah, CEO of Filly Coder (https://fillycoder.com)

Overview:

In this comprehensive guide, Bernard Baah demystifies the world of Python Machine Learning, making it accessible to beginners while offering depth and insights for experienced practitioners. Whether you're a data enthusiast, a programmer, or a professional seeking to harness the potential of machine learning, this book has something for you.

Key Features:

1. **Hands-On Approach:** Bernard believes in learning by doing. Throughout this book, you'll find practical examples, coding exercises, and real-world projects that allow you to apply machine learning concepts immediately.

2. **Comprehensive Coverage:** We start with the fundamentals, introducing you to Python programming and the core concepts of machine learning. From there, we journey through supervised and unsupervised learning, delve into deep learning, and explore natural language processing (NLP), reinforcement learning, and more.

3. **Real-World Applications:** While theory is essential, it's the application that truly matters. We provide case studies, project walkthroughs, and examples from various domains, giving you a taste of how machine learning is transforming industries such as healthcare, finance, and e-commerce.

4. **Ethical Considerations:** We believe in responsible AI. We dedicate a section to ethical considerations in machine learning, addressing issues of bias, fairness, and responsible AI practices.

Who Is This Book For?

- **Beginners:** If you're new to machine learning and Python, this book provides a gentle and structured introduction to both topics, building your skills from the ground up.

- **Intermediate Learners:** For those with some background in machine learning or Python, this book offers an opportunity to deepen your knowledge and tackle more advanced concepts.

- **Professionals:** Professionals seeking to incorporate machine learning into their work will find practical insights and real-world examples to guide their journey.

Why Python?

Python has emerged as the go-to language for machine learning and data science. Its simplicity, vast ecosystem of libraries, and active community make it the perfect choice for both beginners and experienced developers. We leverage Python's power throughout this book, allowing you to harness the full potential of machine learning.

What You'll Learn:

- Build and train machine learning models using Python.

- Explore popular machine learning libraries and frameworks.

- Dive into supervised and unsupervised learning techniques.

- Master deep learning with neural networks and TensorFlow.

- Apply machine learning to real-world problems and projects.

- Understand ethical considerations in AI and machine learning.

Get Started:

Python Machine Learning Essentials, authored by Bernard Baah, CEO of Filly Coder, is designed to be your companion in the exciting journey of mastering machine learning with Python. Each chapter is carefully crafted to build your skills incrementally, leading you from the fundamentals to advanced topics. With hands-on examples, real-world case studies, and ethical insights, this book equips you with the knowledge and skills to excel in the dynamic field of machine learning.

We encourage you to dive in, experiment, and explore. The world of Python Machine Learning Essentials awaits, and Bernard Baah is excited to be your guide on this incredible voyage of discovery.

About the Author

Bernard Baah is a seasoned educator, software developer, and author with a passion for teaching and a wealth of experience in the world of programming and artificial intelligence. With over twelve years of experience teaching a dozen different programming languages and six years focused on teaching Python, Bernard has honed his ability to simplify complex concepts and make them accessible to learners of all levels.

As the CEO of Filly Coder (https://fillycoder.com), Bernard is dedicated to empowering individuals with the knowledge and skills needed to thrive in the fast-paced tech industry. His teaching philosophy centers on hands-on learning, practical problem-solving, and fostering a deep understanding of programming and machine learning concepts.

In addition to Python Machine Learning Essentials, Bernard has authored several books, including "Python Fundamentals," "Python Data Analysis," and "The Use of AI in Software Development." His books and teaching materials have been instrumental in helping countless students and professionals embark on successful programming and AI journeys.

Bernard's expertise extends to web development, data science, and software engineering. He is a firm advocate of responsible AI practices and ethical considerations in technology. His commitment to lifelong learning and staying at the forefront of emerging technologies ensures that his readers and students receive up-to-date and relevant information.

When he's not teaching, coding, or writing, Bernard enjoys exploring the outdoors, seeking inspiration in nature, and occasionally trying his hand at creative writing. He believes that the combination of technical skills and creative thinking is a powerful force for innovation.

Bernard Baah welcomes you to join him on the journey of Python Machine Learning Essentials and hopes to inspire you to explore the endless possibilities of Python and machine learning.

You can connect with Bernard on LinkedIn and follow his work on Filly Coder.

Expanded Table of Contents

1. Introduction to Machine Learning:

- Definition and types of machine learning (supervised, unsupervised, reinforcement learning)

- Historical context and evolution

2. Python Basics:

- Basics of Python programming for machine learning

- Data types, control structures, and functions

3. Libraries and Frameworks:

- Introduction to popular machine learning libraries (NumPy, Pandas, Scikit-learn, TensorFlow, PyTorch, etc.)

- Installation and setup

4. Data Preprocessing:

- Data cleaning and handling missing values

- Feature scaling and normalization

- Handling categorical data

- Data transformation techniques

5. Exploratory Data Analysis (EDA):

- Descriptive statistics

- Data visualization with Matplotlib and Seaborn

- Correlation and feature importance analysis

6. Supervised Learning:

- Regression and classification algorithms

- Model training, evaluation, and validation

- Overfitting and underfitting

7. Unsupervised Learning:

- Clustering algorithms (K-means, hierarchical clustering, DBSCAN)
- Dimensionality reduction techniques (PCA, t-SNE)

8. Ensemble Learning:

- Bagging and boosting techniques
- Random Forests, Gradient Boosting

9. Neural Networks and Deep Learning:

- Introduction to neural networks
- Building a simple neural network
- Deep learning frameworks (TensorFlow, PyTorch)

10. Natural Language Processing (NLP): - Basics of text processing - Sentiment analysis, text classification

11. Model Deployment: - Exporting and deploying models - Integration with web applications

12. Reinforcement Learning: - Basics of reinforcement learning - Q-learning, deep reinforcement learning

13. Model Interpretability: - Understanding and interpreting machine learning models - Feature importance and model explanations

14. Advanced Topics: - Transfer learning - AutoML (Automated Machine Learning) - Hyperparameter tuning

15. Case Studies: - Real-world applications and case studies - Walkthroughs of complete machine learning projects

16. Ethical Considerations: - Bias and fairness in machine learning - Responsible AI practices

17. Future Trends: - Emerging trends in machine learning - Ethical AI and responsible AI developments

18. Hands-On Projects: - Including practical projects and exercises for readers to apply their knowledge

Chapter 1. Introduction to Machine Learning

Machine Learning (ML) is a transformative field at the intersection of computer science and statistics, empowering systems to learn and make decisions without explicit programming. This chapter serves as a gateway into the vast landscape of machine learning, laying the foundation for your journey into the world of intelligent algorithms.

1.1 Definition of Machine Learning

At its core, Machine Learning enables computers to learn from data and improve their performance over time. Rather than relying on explicit programming instructions, machine learning systems leverage patterns and statistical models to make predictions or decisions. This adaptability is a key feature that distinguishes machine learning from traditional rule-based programming.

1.2 Types of Machine Learning

Machine Learning can be broadly categorized into three main types:

- **Supervised Learning:** In supervised learning, models are trained on a labeled dataset, where the input data is paired with corresponding output labels. The algorithm learns to map input features to the correct output, making it capable of making predictions on new, unseen data.

- **Unsupervised Learning:** Unsupervised learning deals with unlabeled data. The algorithm explores the inherent structure within the data, identifying patterns, relationships, or clusters without explicit guidance. Common tasks include clustering and dimensionality reduction.

- **Reinforcement Learning:** Inspired by behavioral psychology, reinforcement learning involves an agent interacting with an environment and learning to make decisions to achieve a goal. The agent receives feedback in the form of rewards or penalties, enabling it to optimize its behavior over time.

1.3 Historical Context and Evolution

The roots of machine learning can be traced back to the mid-20th century, with pioneers like Alan Turing contemplating the concept of machines that could learn. However, it wasn't until the digital age that machine learning truly began to flourish.

- **1950s-1960s:** The earliest foundations were laid, with the development of algorithms and models that paved the way for modern machine learning. Researchers explored concepts like neural networks and decision trees.

- **1980s-1990s:** Machine learning faced challenges and criticisms, leading to a period of reduced interest. However, advancements in algorithms and computing power reignited enthusiasm, with the emergence of support vector machines and ensemble methods.

- **2000s-Present:** The explosion of data and computational capabilities marked a new era for machine learning. Deep learning, a subset of ML focused on neural networks, gained prominence, achieving breakthroughs in image recognition, natural language processing, and more.

As we delve deeper into this book, we'll explore the intricacies of each machine learning type, unraveling the algorithms that power intelligent systems and providing you with the tools to embark on your machine learning journey.

Chapter 2. Python Basics

Before diving into the world of machine learning, it's essential to establish a solid foundation in the Python programming language. Python's simplicity, readability, and extensive libraries make it a preferred choice for machine learning practitioners. This chapter serves as a primer, covering the basics of Python programming that will empower you to seamlessly transition into the realm of machine learning.

2.1 Basics of Python Programming for Machine Learning

Python is a versatile, high-level programming language known for its readability and ease of use. Whether you're a beginner or an experienced developer, its syntax and structure provide a welcoming environment for building machine learning models.

Variables and Data Types:

In Python, variables are used to store information. The data type of a variable determines the kind of information it can hold. Common data types include integers, floating-point numbers, strings, lists, and dictionaries.

```
# Variables and Data Types
age = 25          # Integer
height = 5.9      # Float
name = "John"     # String
grades = [90, 85, 92, 78]  # List
```

Control Structures:

Control structures enable you to manage the flow of your program. Python provides if statements for conditional execution, loops for repetitive tasks, and functions for modularizing code.

```
# Control Structures
if age >= 18:
    print("You are an adult.")
else:
    print("You are a minor.")


for grade in grades:
    print("Grade:", grade)


def greet(name):
    print("Hello, " + name + "!")
```

2.2 Data Types, Control Structures, and Functions

Data Types:

Understanding data types is crucial for effective programming. Python supports various data types, including:

- **int:** Integer values (e.g., 5, -3)
- **float:** Floating-point values (e.g., 3.14, -0.5)
- **str:** String values (e.g., "hello", 'Python')
- **list:** Ordered collection of items (e.g., [1, 2, 3])
- **dict:** Key-value pairs (e.g., {'key': 'value'})

Control Structures:

- **if-elif-else:** Conditional statements for decision-making.
- **for and while loops:** Iterative structures for repeated execution.

Functions:

Functions in Python allow you to encapsulate a set of instructions, making your code modular and reusable. Here's an example:

```python
# Function Definition
def square(x):
    return x ** 2


# Function Call
result = square(5)
print("Square:", result)
```

Mastering these Python basics is the first step on your machine learning journey. As we progress, you'll apply these fundamentals to implement machine learning algorithms, manipulate data, and build sophisticated models. Get ready to unleash the power of Python in the realm of artificial intelligence!

If you find that you need additional tutorials or resources on specific topics related to Python programming, data analysis, visualization, or web application development, consider checking out the other books in our series, available on Amazon:

1. **Python Programming Essentials: A Step-by-Step Tutorial**

    - This book provides a comprehensive guide to learning Python from scratch, covering essential programming concepts, syntax, and techniques.

2. **Python Data Analysis Essentials: Practical Techniques for Real-world Applications**

    - Dive deeper into data analysis with Python, learning advanced techniques for manipulating, analyzing, and visualizing data in real-world scenarios.

3. **Python Data Visualization Essentials: A Practical Approach**

   - Explore the world of data visualization in Python, mastering techniques for creating stunning visualizations and gaining insights from your data.

4. **Django Essentials: Building Modern Web Applications**

   - Learn to build web applications using Django, a powerful Python web framework. This book covers everything you need to know to get started with Django development.

5. **Advanced Django: Building Scalable and Secure Web Applications**

   - Take your Django skills to the next level with advanced topics such as building scalable and secure web applications. Learn best practices for Django development and advanced techniques for building robust web applications.

Each book in our series is available on Amazon and is designed to help you master specific aspects of Python programming and web development. Whether you're a beginner or an experienced developer, there's something for everyone in our series of Python tutorials.

Chapter 3. Libraries and Frameworks

To harness the full potential of machine learning, we leverage a rich ecosystem of libraries and frameworks in the Python programming language. This chapter introduces you to the key tools that will empower you to build, train, and deploy machine learning models efficiently.

3.1 Introduction to Popular Machine Learning Libraries

NumPy:

NumPy stands at the core of numerical computing in Python. It provides support for large, multi-dimensional arrays and matrices, along with mathematical functions to operate on these arrays. NumPy is an essential library for handling the data that fuels machine learning models.

Pandas:

Pandas is a versatile data manipulation library built on top of NumPy. It introduces data structures like DataFrames that simplify handling and analyzing structured data. Whether you're cleaning messy datasets or preparing data for modeling, Pandas is an indispensable tool in the machine learning practitioner's toolkit.

Scikit-learn:

Scikit-learn is a comprehensive machine learning library that offers simple and efficient tools for data analysis and modeling. It includes a wide range of algorithms for classification, regression, clustering, and more. Its user-friendly interface makes it an excellent choice for both beginners and experienced data scientists.

TensorFlow and PyTorch:

TensorFlow and PyTorch are deep learning frameworks that have revolutionized the field of neural networks. They provide a flexible platform for building and training deep learning models, with automatic differentiation, GPU acceleration, and extensive community support. Whether you're interested in image recognition, natural language processing, or reinforcement learning, these frameworks are at the forefront of cutting-edge research.

3.2 Installation and Setup

Before diving into the practical implementation of machine learning models, it's crucial to set up your development environment. Let's walk through the installation process for these essential libraries.

Installing NumPy and Pandas:

```
pip install numpy

pip install pandas
```

Installing Scikit-learn:

```
pip install scikit-learn
```

Installing TensorFlow:

```
pip install tensorflow
```

Installing PyTorch:

For CPU:

```
pip install torch
```

For GPU (if available):

```
pip install torch torchvision torchaudio -f
https://download.pytorch.org/whl/cu111/torch_stable.html
```

By installing these libraries, you equip yourself with the tools to explore, analyze, and model data. In the upcoming chapters, we'll delve deeper into each library, exploring their functionalities and demonstrating how they synergize to create powerful machine learning solutions. Get ready to bring your algorithms to life with the magic of these libraries and frameworks!

Chapter 4. Data Preprocessing

Data is the lifeblood of machine learning, and its quality profoundly influences the performance of your models. This chapter is dedicated to the crucial step of data preprocessing, where we'll explore techniques to clean, transform, and prepare your data for the optimal functioning of machine learning algorithms.

4.1 Data Cleaning and Handling Missing Values

Real-world datasets are often messy, containing missing or inconsistent values. Addressing these issues is fundamental to building robust machine learning models.

```
Identifying Missing Values:

import pandas as pd


# Load the dataset

data = pd.read_csv('your_dataset.csv')


# Check for missing values

print(data.isnull().sum())
```

Handling Missing Values:

Depending on the nature and context of the missing data, you can choose to drop incomplete rows, fill in missing values with averages, or employ more sophisticated imputation methods.

```
# Drop rows with missing values

data = data.dropna()


# Fill missing values with the mean
```

```
data['column_name'].fillna(data['column_name'].mean(), inplace=True)
```

4.2 Feature Scaling and Normalization

Machine learning algorithms often benefit from having input features on similar scales. Scaling and normalization ensure that no single feature dominates the learning process.

In the realm of machine learning and data analysis, datasets often contain numerical features that can have widely varying scales. Feature scaling and normalization are techniques employed to ensure that these features contribute equally to the model's training process and prevent issues such as features with larger scales dominating the learning process. In this section, we'll explore the concepts of feature scaling and normalization and understand when and how to apply them.

Feature scaling is the process of standardizing the range of independent variables or features of the data. It brings all features to a similar scale, ensuring that they have a similar impact on the model's learning process. There are various techniques for feature scaling, but two common ones are Min-Max Scaling and Standardization.

Standardization (Z-score normalization):

```
from sklearn.preprocessing import StandardScaler

scaler = StandardScaler()
data_scaled = scaler.fit_transform(data[['feature1', 'feature2']])
```

Normalization is another technique for scaling features. It transforms feature values so that they have a mean of 0 and a standard deviation of 1. This technique assumes that the data follows a normal distribution or is at least approximately normally distributed. Normalization is also referred to as **Z-score scaling** and is calculated using the following formula:

$$X_{standardized} = \frac{X - \mu}{\sigma}$$

Where:

- X is the original feature value.
- μ is the mean of the feature
- σ is the standard deviation of the feature.

Normalization is particularly useful when working with machine learning algorithms that assume that the input data is normally distributed, such as many linear regression and logistic regression models.

Min-Max Scaling:

```
from sklearn.preprocessing import MinMaxScaler


scaler = MinMaxScaler()
data_scaled = scaler.fit_transform(data[['feature1', 'feature2']])
```

Min-Max Scaling is a popular technique in data preprocessing, particularly in the context of machine learning and data analysis. Its purpose is to transform numerical features (variables) in your dataset onto a common scale, typically between 0 and 1. This scaling method is also known as "Normalization" or "Rescaling."

The Min-Max Scaling process involves the following steps:

1. **Selection of Features:** You choose the numerical features in your dataset that you want to scale. These features should have different ranges or units.

2. **Determine the Minimum and Maximum Values:** For each selected feature, you calculate its minimum (min) and maximum (max) values within the dataset.

3. **Apply the Scaling Formula:** For each data point (observation) in the dataset, you apply the following formula to scale the feature:

```
scaled_value = (original_value - min) / (max - min)
```

1. Here, **original_value** is the value of the feature for a specific data point, **min** is the minimum value of that feature across the dataset, and **max** is the maximum value of that feature across the dataset. The result is a scaled value between 0 (when **original_value** equals **min**) and 1 (when **original_value** equals **max**).

2. **Repeat for All Data Points:** You repeat this scaling process for all data points and all selected features in your dataset.

Min-Max Scaling is useful for several reasons:

- **Normalization:** It ensures that all features are on a similar scale, preventing some features from dominating others during machine learning model training. This is important when you're using algorithms that are sensitive to the scale of input features, such as gradient-based optimization algorithms in deep learning.

- **Interpretability:** The scaled values are interpretable because they are within a fixed range (0 to 1). This makes it easier to compare and understand the impact of different features on the model's output.

- **Robustness:** Min-Max Scaling can handle outliers to some extent. Outliers may still get scaled to values close to 0 or 1, but they won't excessively affect the scaling of other data points.

It's important to note that Min-Max Scaling can also be customized to scale features to a different range if needed. Instead of scaling to [0, 1], you can choose a different minimum and maximum range that suits your specific requirements.

Libraries such as Scikit-learn in Python provide built-in functions for performing Min-Max Scaling on your data, making it a straightforward preprocessing step in your machine learning workflow.

Here's a basic example of using Scikit-learn for Min-Max scaling:

```
from sklearn.preprocessing import MinMaxScaler
```

```
# Create a MinMaxScaler object
scaler = MinMaxScaler()


# Fit the scaler to your data and transform the features
scaled_data = scaler.fit_transform(your_data)
```

When to Use Feature Scaling and Normalization

The decision to use feature scaling or normalization depends on the nature of your data and the requirements of the machine learning algorithm you intend to use. Here are some guidelines:

- **Use Min-Max Scaling (Normalization) When:**

    - Features have varying scales.

    - You want to constrain the feature values to a specific range (e.g., [0, 1]).

    - The machine learning algorithm does not assume normal distribution.

- **Use Normalization (Z-Score Scaling) When:**

    - Features are normally distributed or approximately normally distributed.

    - The algorithm you're using assumes normal distribution (e.g., some linear models).

- **Consider Not Scaling When:**

    - Your data is already on a similar scale, and scaling would not significantly affect the model's performance.

    - You are working with tree-based algorithms (e.g., Decision Trees, Random Forests) as they are generally insensitive to feature scaling.

4.3 Handling Categorical Data

In many real-world datasets, you'll encounter categorical variables, which represent discrete categories or labels rather than continuous numerical values. Handling categorical data is a crucial preprocessing step in machine learning, as most algorithms require numerical input. In this section, we'll explore techniques for effectively handling categorical data, including encoding and transformation methods.

4.3.1 One-Hot Encoding

One-hot encoding is a popular technique used to convert categorical variables into a numerical format that can be readily used by machine learning algorithms. It creates binary columns for each category or label, where a "1" indicates the presence of that category, and "0" indicates its absence. Let's consider an example:

Suppose we have a categorical feature "Color" with three possible values: "Red," "Green," and "Blue." One-hot encoding would transform this feature into three binary columns, as follows:

Color_Red	Color_Green	Color_Blue
1	0	0
0	1	0
0	0	1

In Python, libraries like Scikit-learn provide easy-to-use functions for one-hot encoding. Here's a basic example:

```python
from sklearn.preprocessing import OneHotEncoder

# Create a OneHotEncoder object
encoder = OneHotEncoder()
```

```
# Fit and transform the encoder on the categorical data
encoded_data = encoder.fit_transform(your_categorical_data)
```

One-hot encoding is suitable for categorical features with no inherent ordinal relationship among the categories. However, it can increase the dimensionality of the dataset, so it's essential to consider the trade-off between interpretability and computational complexity.

4.3.2 Label Encoding

Label encoding is another technique for handling categorical variables, primarily for cases where there is an ordinal relationship among the categories. In label encoding, each category is assigned a unique integer label. Consider the example of a "Size" feature with categories "Small," "Medium," and "Large." Label encoding would map these categories to integers:

- "Small" -> 0

- "Medium" -> 1

- "Large" -> 2

Label encoding is suitable when there is a clear order or ranking among the categories. It can be performed in Python using libraries like Scikit-learn:

```
from sklearn.preprocessing import LabelEncoder

# Create a LabelEncoder object
encoder = LabelEncoder()

# Fit and transform the encoder on the categorical data
encoded_data = encoder.fit_transform(your_categorical_data)
```

However, it's essential to use label encoding cautiously, as some machine learning algorithms may interpret the encoded values as having ordinal significance when there might not be a meaningful ordinal relationship in reality.

4.3.3 Binary Encoding

Binary encoding combines the advantages of one-hot encoding and label encoding while mitigating their drawbacks. It represents each category as a binary code, similar to one-hot encoding but with a more compact representation. Binary encoding reduces dimensionality compared to one-hot encoding while preserving the ordinal information. It's particularly useful when dealing with high-cardinality categorical features.

Binary encoding can be implemented using libraries like Scikit-learn, or custom encoding functions can be written.

4.3.4 Other Encoding Techniques

Apart from the techniques mentioned above, there are other advanced encoding methods such as target encoding, mean encoding, and frequency encoding, which may be suitable for specific scenarios. These methods consider the target variable or the distribution of values within each category for encoding.

4.3.5 Handling Ordinal Data

When dealing with ordinal categorical data, it's crucial to explicitly define the order or ranking of categories. Label encoding is typically suitable for such cases, as it assigns integer labels based on the specified order.

4.3.6 Avoiding Data Leakage

When performing encoding, it's important to avoid data leakage. Data leakage occurs when information from the target variable is inadvertently included in the encoding process. To prevent this, encoding should be applied only to the training dataset before splitting it into training and testing subsets.

4.4 Data Transformation Techniques

Data transformation techniques involve altering the format, structure, or distribution of the data to improve its suitability for machine learning models. These techniques can enhance the model's performance, address issues like skewness, and uncover hidden patterns in the data. In this section, we'll explore various data transformation techniques commonly used in data preprocessing.

4.4.1 Log Transformation

Log transformation is a valuable technique for handling data that exhibits a skewed distribution. Skewness refers to the asymmetry of data, where the tail of the distribution is stretched in one direction. Log transformation is particularly useful for data with positive skewness, where most values are concentrated on the lower end.

By applying the natural logarithm (or other logarithmic bases) to the data, you can compress the range of large values and expand the range of small values. This helps make the data more symmetrical and approximates a normal distribution. Log-transformed data can be beneficial when working with machine learning algorithms that assume normality.

The formula for log transformation is:

$$X_{transformed} = log_{10}(X)$$

Where:

X is the original feature value.

Log transformation can be applied to individual features or to the entire dataset, depending on the specific requirements of your analysis.

4.4.2 Box-Cox TransformationX

The **Box-Cox transformation** is a generalization of the log transformation that can handle a wider range of data distributions. It applies a power transformation to the data and is defined by the following formula:

$$\begin{cases} \frac{y^{\lambda}-1}{\lambda}, & \text{if } \lambda \neq 0 \\ \ln(y), & \text{if } \lambda = 0 \end{cases}$$

Here, y represents the original data, and λ is the transformation parameter. The Box-Cox transformation automatically selects the best λ value to achieve the closest approximation to a normal distribution.

4.4.3 Binning

Binning is the process of dividing numerical data into discrete intervals or bins. It can be useful for simplifying complex relationships between features and the target variable. For instance, age data can be grouped into bins like "child," "teenager," "adult," and "senior" instead of treating age as a continuous variable.

Binning can make data more interpretable and help reduce the impact of outliers. However, it should be applied judiciously, as it may result in information loss if not done carefully.

4.4.4 Feature Scaling Revisited

While we discussed feature scaling in the previous section as a means of preparing data for machine learning models, it can also be considered a data transformation technique. Rescaling features using techniques like Min-Max scaling and standardization can help algorithms converge faster and perform better.

4.4.5 Polynomial Features

Polynomial features are a way to introduce non-linearity into linear models. By creating higher-order polynomial terms from the original features, you can capture more complex relationships between variables. Polynomial regression is an example of a technique that utilizes polynomial features.

For example, if you have a single feature X and you generate polynomial features of degree 2, you would add features X^2, X^3, and so on, allowing the model to fit a quadratic or higher-order curve.

4.4.6 Interaction Features

Interaction features involve creating new features based on the interaction between existing features. These features can capture synergistic relationships that may be missed by individual features. Interaction features can be particularly useful in tree-based models and linear regression.

For example, if you have two features X_1 and X_2, you can create an interaction feature $X_1 * X_2$ to account for their combined effect.

4.4.7 Scaling and Centering

Scaling and centering involve transforming numerical features to have a specific mean and standard deviation. This can be beneficial when working with algorithms that are sensitive to feature scales, such as support vector machines.

These techniques adjust feature values to have a mean of 0 and a standard deviation of 1. By centering the data at 0, they remove the bias introduced by the mean, and by scaling to a standard deviation of 1, they ensure that the features have consistent scales.

4.4.8 Dimensionality Reduction

While we'll delve deeper into dimensionality reduction techniques in a later chapter, it's worth mentioning them here. **Dimensionality reduction** methods like Principal Component Analysis (PCA) and t-Distributed Stochastic Neighbor Embedding (t-SNE) transform high-dimensional data into lower-dimensional representations, helping to reduce noise, improve visualization, and speed up computation.

Dimensionality reduction can be especially valuable when dealing with datasets with many features or when preparing data for visualization purposes.

Practice Exercises for Chapter 4: Data Preprocessing:

1. **Data Cleaning:**

   - Write a Python function to handle missing values in a DataFrame. Test it on a dataset with missing values and verify that missing values are appropriately handled.

   - Identify and remove duplicate records from a dataset using Pandas.

2. **Feature Scaling and Normalization:**

   - Implement Min-Max scaling and Z-score normalization functions from scratch using NumPy. Apply these functions to scale features in a given dataset.

   - Explore the effects of feature scaling on different machine learning models by comparing their performance with and without scaling on a regression or classification task.

3. **Handling Categorical Data:**

   - Encode categorical variables using one-hot encoding and label encoding techniques. Apply these encodings to categorical features in a dataset and analyze their impact on model performance.

   - Implement custom encoding methods for handling categorical variables, such as frequency encoding or target encoding, and compare their performance with traditional encoding techniques.

4. **Data Transformation Techniques:**

   - Explore various data transformation techniques, such as log transformation, box-cox transformation, or feature binning, on a dataset with skewed features. Analyze the effect of each transformation on the distribution of the data.

   - Implement a pipeline to automate the data preprocessing steps, including data cleaning, feature scaling, encoding, and transformation. Apply the pipeline to a dataset and evaluate its effectiveness in preparing the data for machine learning models.

Chapter 5. Exploratory Data Analysis (EDA): Descriptive Statistics

Exploratory Data Analysis (EDA) is an essential step in the data analysis process, where the primary objective is to understand the dataset's characteristics and uncover insights. Descriptive statistics play a crucial role in EDA by providing a summary of the dataset's key features and distributions. In this section, we'll explore the concept of descriptive statistics and how they can be applied during EDA.

5.1 What Are Descriptive Statistics?

Descriptive statistics are numerical and graphical techniques used to summarize and describe the main characteristics of a dataset. They provide a concise overview of key data attributes, allowing data analysts and scientists to grasp the dataset's central tendencies, variability, and distribution patterns. Descriptive statistics help answer fundamental questions about the data, such as:

- What are the central values (e.g., mean, median) of the variables?

- How spread out or concentrated are the data points?

- Are there any outliers or extreme values in the dataset?

- What is the shape of the data distribution?

5.1.2 Common Descriptive Statistics

Let's explore some common descriptive statistics and how they contribute to understanding a dataset:

5.1.3 Measures of Central Tendency

- **Mean (Average):** The mean is the sum of all data points divided by the number of data points. It represents the central value of the data and is sensitive to outliers.

- **Median (Middle Value):** The median is the middle value when data points are sorted in ascending order. It is less affected by outliers and is a measure of central tendency.

- **Mode (Most Frequent Value):** The mode is the value that appears most frequently in the dataset. A dataset can have multiple modes or no mode at all.

5.1.4 Measures of Variability

- **Variance:** Variance quantifies how much individual data points deviate from the mean. A high variance indicates greater spread, while a low variance implies data points are closely clustered around the mean.

- **Standard Deviation:** The standard deviation is the square root of the variance. It provides a measure of the average deviation from the mean and is often used to assess data dispersion.

5.1.5 Measures of Distribution

- **Skewness:** Skewness measures the asymmetry of the data distribution. A positive skew indicates a long tail to the right (right-skewed), while a negative skew suggests a long tail to the left (left-skewed).

- **Kurtosis:** Kurtosis measures the "tailedness" of the data distribution. High kurtosis indicates heavy tails and potentially more extreme values, while low kurtosis suggests lighter tails.

5.1.6 Visualizing Descriptive Statistics

In addition to numerical summaries, visualizations are invaluable in EDA. Histograms, box plots, and density plots are common tools for visualizing descriptive statistics. These visualizations provide insights into the distribution, central tendency, and spread of data.

5.1.7 Histograms

Histograms display the frequency or count of data points within predefined bins or intervals. They offer a visual representation of data distribution, making it easy to identify modes, skewness, and potential outliers.

5.1.8 Box Plots

Box plots, also known as box-and-whisker plots, display the five-number summary of a dataset: minimum, first quartile (Q1), median (Q2), third quartile (Q3), and maximum. Box plots help visualize the spread and identify outliers in the data.

5.1.9 Interpreting Descriptive Statistics

Interpreting descriptive statistics is an essential skill for data analysts and data scientists. By examining measures of central tendency, variability, and distribution, you can gain a deeper understanding of your dataset's characteristics. Descriptive statistics also serve as a foundation for subsequent analyses, model building, and decision-making in the data science workflow.

5.1.10 Practical Application

During EDA, analysts often compute and visualize descriptive statistics for each relevant variable in the dataset. This exploration helps identify potential data issues, assess data quality, and inform decisions about preprocessing and modeling strategies.

5.2 Data Visualization with Matplotlib and Seaborn

Effective data visualization is a powerful tool in the data analysis toolkit. It allows you to convey complex information, discover patterns, and gain insights from your data more easily. In this section, we'll explore data visualization using two popular Python libraries: Matplotlib and Seaborn.

5.2.1 Matplotlib

Matplotlib is a widely used data visualization library that provides a flexible and extensive framework for creating static, animated, and interactive visualizations in Python. It offers a wide range of plot types, customization options, and compatibility with various file formats.

Line Plot

```
import matplotlib.pyplot as plt


# Sample data
x = [1, 2, 3, 4, 5]
```

```python
y = [10, 15, 13, 18, 22]

# Create a line plot
plt.plot(x, y)

# Add labels and a title
plt.xlabel('X-axis')
plt.ylabel('Y-axis')
plt.title('Line Plot')

# Display the plot
plt.show()
```

Scatter Plot

```python
import matplotlib.pyplot as plt

# Sample data
x = [1, 2, 3, 4, 5]
y = [10, 15, 13, 18, 22]

# Create a scatter plot
plt.scatter(x, y)

# Add labels and a title
```

```
plt.xlabel('X-axis')

plt.ylabel('Y-axis')

plt.title('Scatter Plot')


# Display the plot

plt.show()
```

5.2.2 Seaborn

Seaborn is built on top of Matplotlib and provides a high-level interface for creating informative and attractive statistical graphics. It simplifies the process of creating complex visualizations and is especially useful for visualizing relationships between variables.

Pair Plot

```
import seaborn as sns

import matplotlib.pyplot as plt


# Load a sample dataset

iris = sns.load_dataset("iris")


# Create a pair plot

sns.pairplot(iris, hue="species")


# Display the plot

plt.show()
```

Heatmap

```
import seaborn as sns
import matplotlib.pyplot as plt


# Create a sample correlation matrix
correlation_matrix = iris.corr()


# Create a heatmap
sns.heatmap(correlation_matrix, annot=True, cmap="coolwarm")


# Add a title
plt.title("Correlation Heatmap")


# Display the plot
plt.show()
```

5.2.3 Choosing the Right Visualization

Selecting the appropriate visualization for your data and the insights you want to convey is essential. Matplotlib and Seaborn offer a variety of plot types, including bar plots, histograms, box plots, violin plots, and more. Your choice of visualization should consider the data's nature, the relationships you want to explore, and the story you want to tell.

5.2.4 Customization and Styling

Both Matplotlib and Seaborn provide extensive customization options to tailor your visualizations to specific needs. You can control aspects such as colors, markers, labels, and axes properties to create visually appealing and informative plots.

5.2.5 Interactivity

While Matplotlib is primarily focused on static visualizations, there are libraries like Plotly that offer interactivity for exploring data through zooming, panning, and tooltips. These interactive visualizations can be valuable when dealing with large datasets or when you want to create web-based dashboards.

5.2.6 Best Practices

When creating data visualizations, it's important to follow best practices for clarity and effectiveness. Ensure that your visualizations have appropriate labels, legends, and titles. Use color schemes that are easy to interpret, and consider the audience for your visualizations.

5.2.7 Practical Application

Data visualization is a crucial step in the exploratory data analysis process. It allows you to gain insights, identify trends, and communicate your findings effectively. Whether you're preparing data for modeling, presenting results, or exploring patterns, Matplotlib and Seaborn are versatile tools for creating informative and visually appealing plots.

Certainly! Here's content for the "Correlation and Feature Importance Analysis" section:

5.3 Correlation and Feature Importance Analysis

Understanding the relationships between features and their impact on the target variable is a crucial aspect of exploratory data analysis (EDA). In this section, we'll delve into correlation analysis and feature importance analysis—two techniques that help assess the significance of features in your dataset.

5.3.1 Correlation Analysis

Correlation analysis measures the statistical relationship between pairs of variables. It quantifies the degree to which one variable changes as another variable changes. Correlation can be a valuable tool for identifying potential associations and dependencies in your data. The most common correlation metric is the Pearson correlation coefficient, which measures linear relationships between variables.

Pearson Correlation Coefficient

The Pearson correlation coefficient, often denoted as r, ranges from -1 to 1:

- $r = 1$ indicates a perfect positive linear correlation.

- $r = -1$ indicates a perfect negative linear correlation.

- $r = 0$ suggests no linear correlation.

```python
import pandas as pd

# Sample data
data = {'Feature1': [1, 2, 3, 4, 5],
        'Feature2': [5, 4, 3, 2, 1]}

# Create a DataFrame
df = pd.DataFrame(data)

# Calculate the Pearson correlation coefficient
correlation = df['Feature1'].corr(df['Feature2'])

# Display the correlation coefficient
print(f"Pearson Correlation Coefficient: {correlation}")
```

Positive correlations suggest that as one feature increases, the other tends to increase as well. Negative correlations indicate that as one feature increases, the other tends to decrease. A correlation close to 0 suggests little to no linear relationship.

5.3.2 Feature Importance Analysis

Feature importance analysis is often applied in the context of machine learning models, particularly for tasks like regression and classification. It helps identify which features contribute most to the model's predictive power. Understanding feature importance can guide feature selection, dimensionality reduction, and model optimization.

Feature Importance in Tree-Based Models

Tree-based models like Decision Trees, Random Forests, and Gradient Boosting provide a built-in mechanism for calculating feature importance. Feature importance scores represent the contribution of each feature to the model's decision-making process.

```python
from sklearn.ensemble import RandomForestRegressor

# Sample data
X = df[['Feature1', 'Feature2']]
y = [10, 15, 13, 18, 22]

# Create a Random Forest Regressor
rf_model = RandomForestRegressor()

# Fit the model to the data
rf_model.fit(X, y)

# Get feature importance scores
importance_scores = rf_model.feature_importances_
```

```
# Display feature importance scores
print("Feature Importance Scores:")
for feature, score in zip(X.columns, importance_scores):
    print(f"{feature}: {score}")
```

Feature importance scores are typically normalized to sum to 1, making them interpretable as percentages of importance.

5.3.3 Practical Applications

- **Correlation Analysis:** Correlation analysis can help identify pairs of features that are highly correlated, which may indicate redundancy in your dataset. Removing redundant features can simplify models and reduce multicollinearity issues.

- **Feature Importance Analysis:** Feature importance analysis guides feature selection and model optimization. By focusing on the most important features, you can potentially achieve better model performance and interpretability.

- **Visualization:** Visualizations like heatmaps and feature importance plots can be powerful tools for conveying relationships and feature importance to stakeholders and decision-makers.

5.3.4 Caveats and Considerations

- Correlation does not imply causation. A high correlation between two variables does not necessarily mean that one causes the other.

- Feature importance is model-dependent. Different algorithms may yield different feature importance scores. It's essential to choose an appropriate model and evaluation metric for your specific problem.

- Overfitting can lead to misleading feature importance scores. Ensure that your model is not overfitting the training data, as this can result in inflated feature importance.

5.3.5 Summary

Correlation and feature importance analysis are valuable techniques in exploratory data analysis and machine learning. They provide insights into the relationships between features and their impact on predictions. By using these techniques wisely, you can make informed decisions about feature selection, model building, and data preprocessing.

Practice Exercises for Chapter 5: Exploratory Data Analysis (EDA):

1. **Descriptive Statistics:**

   - Calculate the mean, median, mode, and standard deviation for each numerical feature in a given dataset using Pandas.

   - Explore the distribution of numerical features by creating histograms and box plots for each feature. Analyze the central tendency, spread, and skewness of the data.

2. **Data Visualization with Matplotlib and Seaborn:**

   - Create scatter plots to visualize the relationship between pairs of numerical features in a dataset. Explore correlations and patterns in the data.

   - Generate bar plots or count plots to visualize the distribution of categorical features. Identify the frequency of different categories and their proportions.

3. **Correlation Analysis:**

   - Compute the correlation matrix for numerical features in a dataset and visualize it using a heatmap. Identify highly correlated features and potential multicollinearity issues.

   - Use pair plots or scatter matrix plots to visualize pairwise relationships between numerical features. Analyze the strength and direction of correlations between variables.

4. **Feature Importance Analysis:**

   - Perform feature importance analysis using techniques such as information gain, Gini impurity, or permutation importance. Identify the most important features for predicting the target variable in a classification or regression problem.

- Utilize feature importance scores from tree-based models (e.g., Random Forest, Gradient Boosting) to rank features and select the most relevant ones for model training.

5. **Interactive Visualizations:**

- Explore interactive visualization libraries such as Plotly or Bokeh to create interactive plots and dashboards for exploring the dataset. Include features such as tooltips, zooming, and filtering to enhance interactivity.

6. **Advanced Visualization Techniques:**

- Experiment with advanced visualization techniques such as 3D plots, parallel coordinates plots, or dendrogram plots for hierarchical clustering. Use these techniques to gain deeper insights into complex datasets.

Chapter 6. Supervised Learning: Regression and Classification Algorithms

Supervised learning is a fundamental branch of machine learning where the model learns from labeled training data to make predictions or decisions based on input features. It can be categorized into two main types: regression and classification. In this section, we'll explore both regression and classification algorithms and their applications.

6.1 Regression Algorithms

Regression is a supervised learning task where the goal is to predict a continuous numerical value, such as stock prices, temperature, or sales revenue. Various regression algorithms exist, each suited to different types of data and assumptions about the relationship between features and the target variable. Here are a few commonly used regression algorithms:

6.1.1 Linear Regression

Linear regression is one of the simplest regression algorithms. It assumes a linear relationship between the features and the target variable. The model aims to fit a straight line to the data, minimizing the sum of squared errors.

```
from sklearn.linear_model import LinearRegression


# Create a Linear Regression model

model = LinearRegression()


# Fit the model to the data

model.fit(X_train, y_train)


# Make predictions
```

```
y_pred = model.predict(X_test)
```

6.1.2 Decision Tree Regression

Decision tree regression models the data as a hierarchical tree structure. Each internal node represents a decision based on a feature, and each leaf node represents a prediction. Decision tree regressors are versatile and can capture non-linear relationships.

```
from sklearn.tree import DecisionTreeRegressor


# Create a Decision Tree Regression model

model = DecisionTreeRegressor()


# Fit the model to the data

model.fit(X_train, y_train)


# Make predictions

y_pred = model.predict(X_test)
```

6.2 Classification Algorithms

Classification is another type of supervised learning, where the goal is to predict a categorical label or class. Classification is widely used in various applications, including spam detection, image recognition, and medical diagnosis. Here are some commonly used classification algorithms:

6.2.1 Logistic Regression

Logistic regression is a classic binary classification algorithm that models the probability of an instance belonging to a particular class. It's widely used for tasks like email classification (spam or not spam) and medical diagnosis (disease or no disease).

```
from sklearn.linear_model import LogisticRegression


# Create a Logistic Regression model
model = LogisticRegression()


# Fit the model to the data
model.fit(X_train, y_train)


# Make predictions
y_pred = model.predict(X_test)
```

6.2.3 Random Forest Classification

Random Forest classification is an ensemble learning method that combines multiple decision trees to make predictions. It's known for its robustness and ability to handle complex datasets.

```
from sklearn.ensemble import RandomForestClassifier


# Create a Random Forest Classification model
model = RandomForestClassifier()


# Fit the model to the data
model.fit(X_train, y_train)


# Make predictions
y_pred = model.predict(X_test)
```

6.2.4 Application Areas

- **Regression**: Regression algorithms are applied in areas like finance for predicting stock prices, in healthcare for estimating patient outcomes, and in real estate for property price predictions.

- **Classification**: Classification algorithms find applications in spam email detection, sentiment analysis of text data, image classification, and medical diagnosis, among many others.

6.2.5 Model Evaluation and Validation

In supervised learning, it's essential to assess the performance of the trained models. Evaluation metrics vary based on the type of task (regression or classification) and specific goals. Common metrics for regression include mean squared error (MSE) and R-squared (R^2), while classification metrics include accuracy, precision, recall, F1 score, and ROC curves.

```
from sklearn.metrics import mean_squared_error, accuracy_score


# Regression evaluation

mse = mean_squared_error(y_true, y_pred)


# Classification evaluation

accuracy = accuracy_score(y_true, y_pred)
```

6.2.6 Choosing the Right Algorithm

Selecting the appropriate algorithm for your supervised learning task depends on various factors, including the nature of the data, the complexity of the problem, and the interpretability of the model. It often involves experimentation and comparing the performance of different algorithms.

6.2.7 Summary

Supervised learning encompasses both regression and classification tasks, allowing you to make predictions or decisions based on labeled data. By understanding and applying regression and classification algorithms, you can tackle a wide range of real-world problems and make data-driven decisions.

6.2.8 Application Areas

- **Regression**: Regression algorithms are applied in areas like finance for predicting stock prices, in healthcare for estimating patient outcomes, and in real estate for property price predictions.

- **Classification**: Classification algorithms find applications in spam email detection, sentiment analysis of text data, image classification, and medical diagnosis, among many others.

6.2.9 Model Evaluation and Validation

In supervised learning, it's essential to assess the performance of the trained models. Evaluation metrics vary based on the type of task (regression or classification) and specific goals. Common metrics for regression include mean squared error (MSE) and R-squared (R^2), while classification metrics include accuracy, precision, recall, F1 score, and ROC curves.

```
from sklearn.metrics import mean_squared_error, accuracy_score


# Regression evaluation

mse = mean_squared_error(y_true, y_pred)


# Classification evaluation

accuracy = accuracy_score(y_true, y_pred)
```

6.2.10 Choosing the Right Algorithm

Selecting the appropriate algorithm for your supervised learning task depends on various factors, including the nature of the data, the complexity of the problem, and the interpretability of the model. It often involves experimentation and comparing the performance of different algorithms.

6.2.11 Summary

Supervised learning encompasses both regression and classification tasks, allowing you to make predictions or decisions based on labeled data. By understanding and applying regression and classification algorithms, you can tackle a wide range of real-world problems and make data-driven decisions.

6.3 Model Training, Evaluation, and Validation

In supervised learning, the process of building and deploying machine learning models involves several critical steps: training, evaluation, and validation. These steps are essential for ensuring that your model performs well on unseen data and generalizes effectively to make reliable predictions.

6.3.1 Model Training

Model training is the initial phase where you teach your machine learning model to make predictions by exposing it to labeled training data. During training, the model learns the underlying patterns and relationships between input features and the target variable. The training process typically involves the following steps:

1. **Data Preparation:** Preprocess and prepare your training dataset. This includes handling missing values, feature scaling, encoding categorical variables, and splitting the data into training and validation sets.

2. **Algorithm Selection:** Choose an appropriate machine learning algorithm for your task. Depending on whether it's a regression or classification problem, you'll select the corresponding algorithm.

3. **Model Fitting:** Train the selected model on the training data. The model adjusts its parameters to minimize the error between its predictions and the actual target values.

```
# Example of model training (classification)
from sklearn.linear_model import LogisticRegression
```

```
# Create a Logistic Regression model
model = LogisticRegression()

# Fit the model to the training data
model.fit(X_train, y_train)
```

4. **Hyperparameter Tuning:** Fine-tune the model's hyperparameters to optimize its performance. This can involve methods like grid search or random search.

6.3.2 Model Evaluation

Once the model is trained, it's crucial to assess its performance using **model evaluation** techniques. Evaluation helps you understand how well the model is likely to perform on unseen data. Evaluation metrics differ depending on the type of problem (regression or classification) and the specific goals of your analysis.

For regression tasks, common evaluation metrics include **Mean Squared Error (MSE)** and **R-squared (R²)**, which measure the accuracy of numerical predictions.

For classification tasks, evaluation metrics include **accuracy, precision, recall, F1 score, ROC curves**, and **confusion matrices**. These metrics provide insights into how well the model can classify instances into different categories.

```
# Example of model evaluation (classification)
from sklearn.metrics import accuracy_score, classification_report,
confusion_matrix

# Make predictions on the validation data
y_pred = model.predict(X_val)

# Calculate accuracy
```

```
accuracy = accuracy_score(y_val, y_pred)


# Generate a classification report

classification_report = classification_report(y_val, y_pred)


# Create a confusion matrix

confusion_matrix = confusion_matrix(y_val, y_pred)
```

6.3.3 Model Validation

Model validation is the process of assessing the model's performance on a separate dataset that it has never seen before. This dataset, known as the validation set, helps you gauge the model's ability to generalize to new, unseen data. Common techniques for validation include cross-validation and holdout validation:

- **Cross-Validation:** In k-fold cross-validation, the dataset is divided into k subsets. The model is trained and evaluated k times, with each subset serving as the validation set once. This helps obtain a more robust estimate of the model's performance.

- **Holdout Validation:** In holdout validation, the dataset is split into training and validation sets. The model is trained on the training set and evaluated on the validation set.

```
from sklearn.model_selection import train_test_split


# Split the data into training and validation sets

X_train, X_val, y_train, y_val = train_test_split(X, y, test_size=0.2,
random_state=42)
```

6.3.4 Overfitting and Underfitting

Overfitting and underfitting are common challenges in machine learning:

- **Overfitting:** Occurs when a model learns the training data too well, capturing noise and irrelevant patterns. It performs well on the training data but poorly on new data.

- **Underfitting:** Occurs when a model is too simple to capture the underlying patterns in the data. It performs poorly on both the training and validation data.

Validation helps detect overfitting and underfitting. If a model performs significantly better on the training data than on the validation data, it may be overfitting.

6.3.5 Summary

In the realm of supervised learning, model training, evaluation, and validation are essential steps in building reliable machine learning models. These processes ensure that your models generalize well to unseen data and make accurate predictions in real-world scenarios. By selecting appropriate algorithms, evaluating performance, and validating models, you can effectively harness the power of supervised learning.

6.4 Overfitting and Underfitting

Overfitting and underfitting are common challenges in machine learning that can significantly impact the performance and generalization of your models. In this section, we'll explore what these phenomena are, how to identify them, and strategies to mitigate them.

6.4.1 Overfitting

Overfitting occurs when a machine learning model learns the training data too well, capturing not only the underlying patterns but also noise and random fluctuations. As a result, the model becomes too complex and adapts too closely to the training data, making it less effective at making predictions on new, unseen data.

Signs of Overfitting:

- The model's performance on the training data is excellent, with a low training error.

- However, the model's performance on validation or test data is significantly worse, with a higher error or lower accuracy.

Causes of Overfitting:

- Using an excessively complex model with too many features or parameters.

- Collecting insufficient training data that may not represent the true underlying distribution.

- Failure to apply regularization techniques or constraints on the model.

Mitigation Strategies for Overfitting:

1. **Simplify the Model:** Consider using a simpler model with fewer features or parameters to reduce complexity.

2. **Feature Selection:** Identify and select the most relevant features while excluding irrelevant ones.

3. **Regularization:** Apply regularization techniques like L1 or L2 regularization to penalize large parameter values and encourage a simpler model.

4. **Cross-Validation:** Use cross-validation to assess the model's performance on multiple subsets of the data and detect overfitting.

6.4.2 Underfitting

Underfitting occurs when a machine learning model is too simple to capture the underlying patterns in the data. In such cases, the model fails to fit the training data adequately and performs poorly on both the training and validation/test data.

Signs of Underfitting:

- The model's performance on both the training data and validation/test data is subpar, with a high error or low accuracy.

Causes of Underfitting:

- Using an overly simple model that lacks the capacity to capture the data's complexity.

- Insufficient model training, such as too few training iterations or epochs.

- Poor feature selection or feature engineering.

Mitigation Strategies for Underfitting:

1. **Use a More Complex Model:** Consider using a more complex model with additional features or layers.

2. **Feature Engineering:** Improve feature engineering to provide the model with more relevant information.

3. **Increase Training:** Train the model for more epochs or iterations to allow it to learn the data better.

4. **Collect More Data:** Collect more training data to provide the model with a richer dataset.

6.4.3 Balancing Overfitting and Underfitting

Finding the right balance between overfitting and underfitting is crucial for building effective machine learning models. This balance depends on the specific problem, the dataset, and the chosen algorithm. The goal is to create a model that generalizes well to unseen data while avoiding unnecessary complexity.

Validation Curves: Validation curves can help visualize the trade-off between model complexity and performance. They show how a model's performance changes as you vary hyperparameters or model complexity.

Learning Curves: Learning curves display the training and validation performance as a function of the training dataset's size. They help determine if a model would benefit from more data.

6.4.4 Summary

Overfitting and underfitting are common challenges in machine learning that can impact the performance and reliability of your models. Identifying the signs and understanding the causes of these phenomena is essential for building models that generalize well to new data. By striking the right balance between model complexity, training data, and regularization, you can create machine learning models that make accurate predictions in real-world scenarios.

Practice Exercises for Chapter 6: Supervised Learning:

1. **Regression:**

   - Implement a simple linear regression model from scratch using NumPy. Train the model on a small dataset and evaluate its performance using mean squared error or R-squared.

   - Explore different regression algorithms such as Ridge Regression, Lasso Regression, or Polynomial Regression using Scikit-learn. Train each model on a dataset and compare their performance.

2. **Classification:**

   - Train a basic classification model (e.g., Logistic Regression) on a real-world dataset such as the Iris dataset or the Breast Cancer dataset from Scikit-learn. Evaluate the model's performance using metrics like accuracy, precision, recall, and F1-score.

   - Experiment with different classification algorithms such as Decision Trees, Random Forests, Support Vector Machines (SVM), or k-Nearest Neighbors (k-NN). Compare the performance of these algorithms on the same dataset.

3. **Model Evaluation:**

   - Implement cross-validation techniques such as k-fold cross-validation or stratified cross-validation to evaluate the generalization performance of a model. Use different values of k and compare the results.

   - Explore different evaluation metrics for regression models (e.g., mean squared error, mean absolute error) and classification models (e.g., accuracy, precision, recall, F1-score). Calculate these metrics for a trained model and interpret the results.

4. **Hyperparameter Tuning:**

- Perform hyperparameter tuning for a classification or regression model using techniques such as grid search or random search. Search for optimal hyperparameters and assess the impact on model performance.

- Experiment with automated hyperparameter tuning libraries such as Hyperopt or Bayesian Optimization to find the best hyperparameters for a given model and dataset.

5. **Model Selection:**

- Implement model selection techniques such as nested cross-validation or model ensembles to choose the best model from a set of candidate models. Evaluate the performance of each model and select the one with the highest performance.

Chapter 7. Unsupervised Learning: Clustering Algorithms

Unsupervised learning is a branch of machine learning where the goal is to uncover patterns and structures within data without the presence of labeled target variables. Clustering algorithms are a fundamental component of unsupervised learning and are used to group similar data points together. In this section, we'll explore some of the most commonly used clustering algorithms, including K-means, hierarchical clustering, and DBSCAN.

7.1 K-means Clustering

K-means clustering is one of the most popular and straightforward clustering algorithms. It divides a dataset into K clusters based on the similarity of data points. Here's how it works:

1. **Initialization:** Choose K initial cluster centroids randomly from the data.

2. **Assignment:** Assign each data point to the nearest centroid, forming K clusters.

3. **Update Centroids:** Recalculate the centroids of each cluster based on the data points assigned to them.

4. **Repeat:** Repeat steps 2 and 3 until convergence (when centroids no longer change significantly) or a predetermined number of iterations.

```
from sklearn.cluster import KMeans


# Create a K-means clustering model with K clusters

kmeans = KMeans(n_clusters=K)


# Fit the model to the data

kmeans.fit(X)
```

```
# Get cluster assignments for each data point
labels = kmeans.labels_

# Get cluster centroids
centroids = kmeans.cluster_centers_
```

K-means is useful for partitioning data into well-defined clusters when the number of clusters K is known in advance.

7.1.2 Hierarchical Clustering

Hierarchical clustering creates a tree-like structure of clusters, known as a dendrogram, by iteratively merging or splitting clusters. It doesn't require specifying the number of clusters in advance and offers a hierarchical view of data grouping. There are two main types of hierarchical clustering:

- **Agglomerative Hierarchical Clustering:** Starts with individual data points as separate clusters and merges them iteratively based on similarity.

- **Divisive Hierarchical Clustering:** Begins with all data points in a single cluster and recursively divides them into smaller clusters.

```
from sklearn.cluster import AgglomerativeClustering

# Create an Agglomerative Hierarchical Clustering model
agg_clustering = AgglomerativeClustering(n_clusters=K)

# Fit the model to the data
```

```
agg_clustering.fit(X)


# Get cluster assignments for each data point

labels = agg_clustering.labels_
```

Hierarchical clustering is advantageous when the number of clusters is unknown, and you want to explore the data's structure in a hierarchical manner.

7.1.3 DBSCAN (Density-Based Spatial Clustering of Applications with Noise)

DBSCAN is a density-based clustering algorithm that groups data points based on their density and separates regions of different densities. It can identify outliers (noise) and discover clusters of arbitrary shapes. Key concepts in DBSCAN are:

- **Core Points:** Data points with a minimum number of neighbors within a specified radius (density threshold).

- **Border Points:** Data points within the radius of a core point but with fewer neighbors than the minimum threshold.

- **Noise Points:** Data points that are neither core nor border points.

```
from sklearn.cluster import DBSCAN


# Create a DBSCAN clustering model

dbscan = DBSCAN(eps=0.5, min_samples=5)


# Fit the model to the data

dbscan.fit(X)


# Get cluster assignments for each data point
```

```
labels = dbscan.labels_
```

DBSCAN is effective for discovering clusters of varying shapes and handling noisy data.

7.1.4 Applications of Clustering

Clustering algorithms find applications in various fields, including:

- **Customer Segmentation:** Segmenting customers based on their behavior and preferences for targeted marketing.

- **Image Segmentation:** Dividing an image into regions with similar characteristics for object detection or image processing.

- **Anomaly Detection:** Identifying outliers and unusual patterns in data.

- **Document Clustering:** Grouping similar documents for content organization and recommendation systems.

7.1.5 Choosing the Right Clustering Algorithm

The choice of clustering algorithm depends on the nature of your data and the goals of your analysis. K-means is suitable for well-defined spherical clusters, hierarchical clustering for hierarchical structures, and DBSCAN for arbitrary-shaped clusters. Experimentation and domain knowledge often guide the selection process.

7.1.6 Summary

Unsupervised learning, specifically clustering algorithms, plays a vital role in uncovering patterns and structures within data without the need for labeled target variables. By understanding and applying clustering techniques like K-means, hierarchical clustering, and DBSCAN, you can gain insights from unlabeled data and make data-driven decisions in various domains.

7.2 Dimensionality Reduction Techniques

In machine learning and data analysis, high-dimensional data can pose challenges such as increased computation time, the curse of dimensionality, and difficulties in visualizing data. Dimensionality reduction techniques aim to address these challenges by reducing the number of features while preserving essential information. In this section, we'll explore two widely used dimensionality reduction techniques: Principal Component Analysis (PCA) and t-Distributed Stochastic Neighbor Embedding (t-SNE).

7.2.1 Principal Component Analysis (PCA)

Principal Component Analysis (PCA) is a linear dimensionality reduction technique that transforms high-dimensional data into a lower-dimensional representation. It achieves this by finding the principal components, which are linear combinations of the original features. These components capture the maximum variance in the data, allowing for dimensionality reduction while retaining as much information as possible.

The steps involved in PCA are as follows:

1. **Standardization:** Standardize the data by subtracting the mean and dividing by the standard deviation for each feature.

2. **Covariance Matrix:** Compute the covariance matrix of the standardized data.

3. **Eigenvalue Decomposition:** Calculate the eigenvalues and eigenvectors of the covariance matrix.

4. **Selecting Principal Components:** Choose the top k eigenvectors (principal components) that explain the most variance. Typically, this is done by sorting the eigenvalues in descending order.

5. **Projection:** Project the data onto the selected principal components to obtain the reduced-dimensional representation.

```
from sklearn.decomposition import PCA


# Create a PCA model with a specified number of components (k)

pca = PCA(n_components=k)
```

```
# Fit the model to the data and transform it
X_pca = pca.fit_transform(X)
```

PCA is useful for data compression, visualization, and noise reduction. It is commonly used in various fields, including image processing, biology, and finance.

7.2.2 t-Distributed Stochastic Neighbor Embedding (t-SNE)

t-Distributed Stochastic Neighbor Embedding (t-SNE) is a non-linear dimensionality reduction technique that is particularly effective for visualizing high-dimensional data in a lower-dimensional space. Unlike PCA, t-SNE focuses on preserving the local structure of data points, making it well-suited for visualizing clusters and patterns.

The key steps in t-SNE are as follows:

1. **Pairwise Similarities:** Compute pairwise similarities between data points in the high-dimensional space, using a Gaussian distribution for similarity.

2. **Student's t-Distribution:** Construct a probability distribution in the lower-dimensional space, aiming to minimize the divergence between the high-dimensional and lower-dimensional distributions.

3. **Gradient Descent:** Optimize the lower-dimensional representation by minimizing the divergence between distributions using gradient descent.

```
from sklearn.manifold import TSNE

# Create a t-SNE model with a specified number of dimensions (usually 2 or 3)
tsne = TSNE(n_components=2)
```

```
# Fit the model to the data and transform it
X_tsne = tsne.fit_transform(X)
```

t-SNE is widely used for visualizing complex, high-dimensional data, such as images, natural language data, and genomic data. It is a valuable tool for exploring data and uncovering patterns that may be challenging to discern in the original high-dimensional space.

7.3 Choosing Between PCA and t-SNE

The choice between PCA and t-SNE depends on your specific goals and the nature of your data:

- **PCA:** Use PCA for linear dimensionality reduction when you need to preserve the global structure of the data, reduce computation time, or compress data for further analysis.

- **t-SNE:** Choose t-SNE for non-linear dimensionality reduction when you want to visualize data in a lower-dimensional space while preserving local structures, uncover clusters, or explore intricate patterns.

Both techniques have their strengths and weaknesses, and the decision should align with the objectives of your analysis.

7.4 Summary

Dimensionality reduction techniques such as PCA and t-SNE play a crucial role in simplifying and visualizing high-dimensional data. By transforming complex data into lower-dimensional representations, these techniques help address challenges related to computation, visualization, and pattern discovery. Whether you choose PCA for linear dimensionality reduction or t-SNE for non-linear visualization, mastering these techniques empowers you to gain insights from high-dimensional datasets effectively.

Practice Exercises for Chapter 7: Unsupervised Learning:

1. **Clustering Algorithms:**

- Implement the K-means clustering algorithm from scratch using NumPy. Apply it to a synthetic dataset and visualize the resulting clusters.

- Explore the performance of different clustering algorithms such as K-means, hierarchical clustering, and DBSCAN on a real-world dataset. Compare their clustering results and evaluate their strengths and weaknesses.

2. **Dimensionality Reduction:**

- Use Principal Component Analysis (PCA) to reduce the dimensionality of a high-dimensional dataset. Visualize the explained variance ratio for each principal component and select the optimal number of components.

- Implement t-SNE (t-distributed Stochastic Neighbor Embedding) to visualize high-dimensional data in a lower-dimensional space. Apply t-SNE to a dataset with complex relationships between features and visualize the resulting clusters.

3. **Clustering Evaluation:**

- Evaluate the quality of clustering results using internal evaluation metrics such as silhouette score, Davies–Bouldin index, or Calinski-Harabasz index. Apply these metrics to assess the performance of different clustering algorithms on a dataset.

- Implement external evaluation metrics such as adjusted Rand index or normalized mutual information to compare clustering results with ground truth labels (if available). Analyze the agreement between clustering results and true labels.

4. **Dimensionality Reduction Techniques Comparison:**

- Compare the performance of PCA and t-SNE on a high-dimensional dataset in terms of visualization quality and clustering results. Analyze the trade-offs between dimensionality reduction techniques and their suitability for different types of data.

5. **Applications of Unsupervised Learning:**

- Apply clustering algorithms to perform customer segmentation on a retail dataset. Identify distinct customer segments based on their purchasing behavior and demographic information.

- Use dimensionality reduction techniques to visualize word embeddings learned from a large text corpus. Analyze semantic similarities between words and explore relationships between different word clusters.

Chapter 8. Ensemble Learning: Bagging and Boosting Techniques

Ensemble learning is a powerful machine learning technique that combines multiple base models (often called "weak learners") to create a stronger, more accurate model. In this section, we'll delve into two popular ensemble learning methods: **Bagging** and **Boosting**.

8.1 Bagging (Bootstrap Aggregating)

Bagging, short for Bootstrap Aggregating, is an ensemble technique that aims to reduce the variance of a machine learning model by averaging or voting the predictions of multiple independently trained base models. The process involves the following steps:

1. **Bootstrap Sampling:** Generate multiple random subsets (with replacement) from the training data. Each subset is called a "bootstrap sample."

2. **Base Model Training:** Train a separate base model on each bootstrap sample. These base models can be any algorithm, such as decision trees or random forests.

3. **Predictions:** For a new data point, obtain predictions from all base models.

4. **Aggregation:** Combine the predictions using averaging (for regression problems) or voting (for classification problems) to make the final ensemble prediction.

Random Forest is a widely known example of a bagging ensemble method. It consists of multiple decision trees, where each tree is trained on a bootstrap sample of the data.

```
from sklearn.ensemble import RandomForestClassifier


# Create a Random Forest classifier
rf_classifier = RandomForestClassifier(n_estimators=100)
```

```
# Fit the model to the training data
rf_classifier.fit(X_train, y_train)


# Make predictions
y_pred = rf_classifier.predict(X_test)
```

Bagging helps reduce overfitting and improves the model's stability by combining the predictions from multiple diverse models.

8.1.2 Boosting

Boosting is another ensemble technique that aims to improve the model's accuracy by training base models sequentially, with each new model focusing on the instances that previous models found difficult to classify. The key idea is to give more weight to misclassified samples, making them more influential in subsequent models. The boosting process typically follows these steps:

1. **Initialize Weights:** Assign equal weights to all training samples.

2. **Base Model Training:** Train a base model on the training data with the current sample weights.

3. **Evaluate Model:** Evaluate the base model's performance on the training data.

4. **Update Weights:** Increase the weights of misclassified samples, making them more influential in the next iteration.

5. **Repeat:** Repeat steps 2-4 for a specified number of iterations or until convergence.

6. **Final Prediction:** Combine the predictions of all base models using weighted voting to make the final ensemble prediction.

AdaBoost (Adaptive Boosting) and **Gradient Boosting** are well-known boosting algorithms, each with its own variation of the boosting process.

```
from sklearn.ensemble import AdaBoostClassifier
```

```
# Create an AdaBoost classifier with a base estimator

adaboost_classifier =
AdaBoostClassifier(base_estimator=DecisionTreeClassifier(max_depth=1)
, n_estimators=50)


# Fit the model to the training data

adaboost_classifier.fit(X_train, y_train)


# Make predictions

y_pred = adaboost_classifier.predict(X_test)
```

Boosting often leads to highly accurate models but can be more prone to overfitting if not controlled properly. Common base estimators used in boosting are decision trees with limited depth.

8.1.3 Choosing Between Bagging and Boosting

The choice between bagging and boosting depends on your specific problem and data characteristics:

- **Bagging:** Use bagging when you want to reduce variance, improve model stability, and prevent overfitting. It works well with high-variance models.

- **Boosting:** Choose boosting when you aim to improve predictive accuracy by focusing on difficult-to-classify instances. It is particularly useful when dealing with biased data or when you want a strong predictive model.

8.1.4 Summary

Ensemble learning techniques like bagging and boosting leverage the power of multiple base models to create stronger, more accurate machine learning models. Bagging reduces variance and enhances stability, while boosting focuses on improving predictive accuracy by giving more weight to challenging instances. Understanding these ensemble methods and when to apply them is essential for building robust and high-performing machine learning models.

8.2 Ensemble Learning: Random Forests and Gradient Boosting

In this section, we'll dive deeper into two popular and highly effective ensemble learning techniques: **Random Forests** and **Gradient Boosting**. These methods leverage the power of multiple base models to create strong and accurate ensemble models, making them invaluable tools in machine learning.

8.2.1 Random Forests

Random Forest is a versatile ensemble learning algorithm that combines the strengths of decision trees with bagging. It builds multiple decision trees during training and combines their predictions through voting or averaging. The key features of Random Forests are as follows:

- **Bootstrap Sampling:** Like bagging, Random Forests create multiple bootstrap samples from the training data to train each decision tree.

- **Feature Randomization:** In addition to sampling data, Random Forests also randomly select a subset of features for each decision tree. This feature randomness decorrelates the trees and reduces overfitting.

- **Voting (Classification) or Averaging (Regression):** For classification problems, the final prediction is made by a majority vote among the decision trees. For regression, the predictions are averaged.

```
from sklearn.ensemble import RandomForestClassifier


# Create a Random Forest classifier
```

```
rf_classifier = RandomForestClassifier(n_estimators=100,
max_depth=None, random_state=42)


# Fit the model to the training data

rf_classifier.fit(X_train, y_train)


# Make predictions

y_pred = rf_classifier.predict(X_test)
```

Random Forests are known for their robustness, scalability, and ability to handle high-dimensional data. They are suitable for both classification and regression tasks and often produce competitive results with minimal hyperparameter tuning.

8.2.2 Gradient Boosting

Gradient Boosting is a powerful ensemble technique that builds multiple decision trees sequentially, with each tree correcting the errors of its predecessor. It is particularly effective in creating strong predictive models. Key components of Gradient Boosting include:

- **Weak Learners:** Gradient Boosting typically uses shallow decision trees (weak learners) as base models, often with a maximum depth of one or two.

- **Gradient Descent:** The algorithm minimizes a loss function (e.g., mean squared error for regression or cross-entropy for classification) by iteratively adjusting the weights of training instances.

- **Learning Rate:** A hyperparameter that controls the step size during optimization. Smaller learning rates lead to more stable but slower convergence.

```
from sklearn.ensemble import GradientBoostingClassifier
```

```
# Create a Gradient Boosting classifier

gb_classifier = GradientBoostingClassifier(n_estimators=100,
learning_rate=0.1, max_depth=3, random_state=42)


# Fit the model to the training data

gb_classifier.fit(X_train, y_train)


# Make predictions

y_pred = gb_classifier.predict(X_test)
```

Gradient Boosting often produces highly accurate models but may require careful tuning of hyperparameters to avoid overfitting. Common implementations of Gradient Boosting include AdaBoost and the more advanced XGBoost and LightGBM libraries.

8.3 Choosing Between Random Forests and Gradient Boosting

The choice between Random Forests and Gradient Boosting depends on your specific problem and objectives:

- **Random Forests:** Use Random Forests when you want a robust and versatile ensemble method that requires minimal hyperparameter tuning. They are well-suited for both classification and regression tasks.

- **Gradient Boosting:** Choose Gradient Boosting when you seek maximum predictive accuracy and are willing to invest time in hyperparameter tuning. Gradient Boosting excels in creating strong predictive models but may be more sensitive to overfitting.

8.4 Summary

Random Forests and Gradient Boosting are powerful ensemble learning techniques that have proven their effectiveness in a wide range of machine learning applications. Whether you opt for the simplicity and robustness of Random Forests or the predictive power of Gradient Boosting, these methods offer valuable tools for building accurate and robust predictive models.

Practice Exercises for Chapter 8: Ensemble Learning:

1. **Bagging Techniques:**

   - Implement a bagging ensemble method such as Random Forest from scratch using decision trees. Train multiple decision tree classifiers on bootstrap samples of the training data and combine their predictions using majority voting or averaging. Compare the performance of the bagging ensemble with a single decision tree on a classification or regression task.

2. **Boosting Techniques:**

   - Implement a boosting ensemble method such as AdaBoost from scratch using decision stumps (weak learners). Train a sequence of weak learners iteratively, where each learner focuses on the instances that were misclassified by the previous ones. Combine the predictions of all weak learners to obtain the final ensemble prediction. Evaluate the performance of AdaBoost on a classification task and compare it with other boosting algorithms like Gradient Boosting.

3. **Random Forest:**

   - Train a Random Forest classifier using Scikit-learn on a real-world dataset such as the Iris dataset or the Breast Cancer dataset. Experiment with different hyperparameters such as the number of trees, maximum depth of trees, and minimum samples per leaf. Evaluate the performance of the Random Forest classifier using cross-validation and compare it with other ensemble methods.

4. **Gradient Boosting:**

   - Implement a Gradient Boosting classifier using a library like XGBoost or LightGBM. Train the Gradient Boosting model on a dataset with a large number of features and instances. Experiment with different boosting parameters such as learning rate, tree depth, and regularization to optimize the model's performance. Evaluate the model's performance on a holdout test set and visualize the feature importance scores.

5. **Ensemble Model Comparison:**

   - Compare the performance of different ensemble methods (e.g., Random Forest, AdaBoost, Gradient Boosting) on multiple datasets with varying characteristics (e.g., size, dimensionality, imbalance). Evaluate the ensemble methods using appropriate evaluation metrics (e.g., accuracy, F1-score, AUC-ROC) and analyze their strengths and weaknesses.

Chapter 9. Neural Networks and Deep Learning: Introduction to Neural Networks

In this section, we will embark on an exciting journey into the world of neural networks and deep learning. Neural networks are at the forefront of artificial intelligence and have enabled groundbreaking advancements in various domains, including computer vision, natural language processing, and robotics.

9.1 What Are Neural Networks?

Neural networks, often referred to as artificial neural networks or simply "neural nets," are computational models inspired by the structure and function of the human brain. They are composed of interconnected nodes, or "neurons," organized into layers. Neural networks are particularly adept at capturing complex patterns and representations in data.

The fundamental components of a neural network include:

- **Input Layer:** The first layer that receives data or features.

- **Hidden Layers:** Intermediate layers that transform the input data through a series of mathematical operations. Deep neural networks have multiple hidden layers.

- **Output Layer:** The final layer that produces the network's prediction or output.

Each connection between neurons has an associated weight, and each neuron typically applies an activation function to its input. Training a neural network involves adjusting these weights to minimize the difference between its predictions and the actual target values.

9.1.2 Why Neural Networks?

Neural networks have gained immense popularity and widespread adoption due to several key advantages:

- **Representation Learning:** Neural networks automatically learn and extract relevant features from the data, eliminating the need for manual feature engineering.

- **Flexibility:** They can model complex, non-linear relationships in data, making them suitable for a wide range of tasks.

- **Scalability:** Deep neural networks, in particular, can scale to handle large and high-dimensional datasets.

- **State-of-the-Art Performance:** Neural networks have achieved state-of-the-art results in image recognition, natural language understanding, and many other areas.

9.1.3 Applications of Neural Networks

Neural networks have revolutionized various fields with their applications, including:

- **Computer Vision:** Convolutional Neural Networks (CNNs) have enabled image recognition, object detection, and facial recognition systems.

- **Natural Language Processing (NLP):** Recurrent Neural Networks (RNNs) and Transformer-based models have transformed language understanding, enabling tasks like machine translation and sentiment analysis.

- **Autonomous Vehicles:** Neural networks power self-driving cars by processing sensor data and making real-time decisions.

- **Healthcare:** They assist in medical image analysis, disease diagnosis, and drug discovery.

- **Gaming:** Reinforcement learning, a subset of deep learning, has been used to master complex games like Go and chess.

9.1.4 Getting Started with Neural Networks

To start your journey into neural networks and deep learning, you'll need to familiarize yourself with deep learning frameworks like **TensorFlow** and **PyTorch**. These frameworks provide the tools and libraries necessary to create, train, and deploy neural networks.

You'll also need to understand key concepts such as loss functions, optimization algorithms (e.g., gradient descent), and the backpropagation algorithm, which is crucial for updating neural network weights during training.

As you delve deeper into this fascinating field, you'll explore various types of neural networks, including feedforward neural networks, convolutional neural networks (CNNs), recurrent neural networks (RNNs), and more.

9.1.5 Summary

In this section, we've introduced the concept of neural networks and their importance in the field of deep learning. Neural networks have revolutionized artificial intelligence by enabling machines to learn and make intelligent decisions from data. As you continue your journey, you'll delve into the intricacies of building and training neural networks for a wide range of applications.

9.2 Neural Networks and Deep Learning: Building a Simple Neural Network

Now that we've introduced the concept of neural networks, it's time to dive deeper and build our own simple neural network. This hands-on section will guide you through the process of creating a basic neural network using Python and a deep learning framework like TensorFlow or PyTorch.

9.2.1 Building Blocks of a Neural Network

Before we start building our neural network, let's understand its fundamental components:

- **Input Layer:** This layer receives the initial data or features for processing. The number of neurons in the input layer corresponds to the number of features in your dataset.

- **Hidden Layers:** These intermediate layers perform mathematical operations on the input data. Each neuron in a hidden layer applies a weighted sum of inputs and an activation function.

- **Output Layer:** The final layer produces the network's prediction or output. The structure and number of neurons in this layer depend on the problem you're solving (e.g., regression or classification).

- **Weights and Biases:** Each connection between neurons has an associated weight, which determines the strength of the connection. Additionally, each neuron has a bias term that influences its output.

9.2.2 Building a Neural Network in TensorFlow

Let's create a simple feedforward neural network using TensorFlow, a popular deep learning framework. We'll build a network to perform binary classification. Here's a step-by-step example:

1. **Import Libraries:**

```python
import tensorflow as tf
from tensorflow import keras
```

2. **Prepare the Dataset:**

Ensure you have your dataset prepared with features (**X**) and corresponding labels (**y**).

3. **Build the Model:**

```python
model = keras.Sequential([
    keras.layers.Dense(128, activation='relu', input_shape=(num_features,)),  # Input layer
    keras.layers.Dense(64, activation='relu'),                # Hidden layer
    keras.layers.Dense(1, activation='sigmoid')               # Output layer (for binary classification)
])
```

Compile the Model:

```python
model.compile(optimizer='adam', loss='binary_crossentropy', metrics=['accuracy'])
```

Train the Model:

```
model.fit(X_train, y_train, epochs=10, batch_size=32,
validation_data=(X_val, y_val))
```

Evaluate the Model:

```
test_loss, test_accuracy = model.evaluate(X_test, y_test)

print(f"Test Loss: {test_loss}, Test Accuracy: {test_accuracy}")
```

9.2.3 Building a Neural Network in PyTorch

Alternatively, you can create a simple neural network using PyTorch, another widely-used deep learning framework. Here's a PyTorch example for binary classification:

1. **Import Libraries:**

```
import torch

import torch.nn as nn

import torch.optim as optim
```

2. **Prepare the Dataset:**

Ensure you have your dataset prepared with features (**X**) and corresponding labels (**y**).

3. **Define the Model:**

```
class SimpleNN(nn.Module):

    def __init__(self, input_size, hidden_size):

        super(SimpleNN, self).__init__()

        self.fc1 = nn.Linear(input_size, hidden_size)

        self.relu = nn.ReLU()

        self.fc2 = nn.Linear(hidden_size, 1)

        self.sigmoid = nn.Sigmoid()
```

```python
    def forward(self, x):

        out = self.fc1(x)

        out = self.relu(out)

        out = self.fc2(out)

        out = self.sigmoid(out)

        return out


model = SimpleNN(input_size=num_features, hidden_size=128)
```

Define the Loss Function and Optimizer:

```python
criterion = nn.BCELoss()

optimizer = optim.Adam(model.parameters(), lr=0.001)
```

Training the Model:

```python
for epoch in range(epochs):

    optimizer.zero_grad()

    outputs = model(X_train)

    loss = criterion(outputs, y_train)

    loss.backward()

    optimizer.step()
```

Evaluating the Model:

```python
with torch.no_grad():

    outputs = model(X_test)

    predicted = (outputs > 0.5).float()
```

```
accuracy = (predicted == y_test).float().mean()

print(f"Test Accuracy: {accuracy.item()}")
```

9.2.4 Summary

In this section, we've taken the first step into building neural networks by creating a simple feedforward network for binary classification using either TensorFlow or PyTorch. Understanding the structure of a neural network, including layers, activation functions, and the training process, is crucial as you explore more complex architectures and tackle real-world problems.

Building and experimenting with neural networks will deepen your understanding of deep learning and prepare you for more advanced topics in the field.

9.3 Neural Networks and Deep Learning: Deep Learning Frameworks (TensorFlow, PyTorch)

In this section, we will explore two of the most prominent deep learning frameworks: **TensorFlow** and **PyTorch**. These frameworks have played a pivotal role in the advancement of deep learning and have gained widespread adoption in both research and industry.

9.3.1 TensorFlow

TensorFlow is an open-source deep learning framework developed by Google Brain. It offers a comprehensive ecosystem for building and deploying machine learning and deep learning models. Some key features and advantages of TensorFlow include:

- **Flexibility:** TensorFlow provides a high-level API (Keras) for quick model prototyping and a lower-level API for fine-grained control over model architecture.

- **Scalability:** It supports both CPU and GPU computation, making it suitable for training models on various hardware platforms.

- **TensorBoard:** TensorFlow comes with TensorBoard, a powerful visualization tool for monitoring and analyzing model training and performance.

- **Community and Resources:** TensorFlow has a vast user community, extensive documentation, and a wealth of pre-trained models available through TensorFlow Hub.

9.3.2 PyTorch

PyTorch, developed by Facebook's AI Research lab (FAIR), is another popular deep learning framework known for its dynamic computational graph and Pythonic design. Key features and advantages of PyTorch include:

- **Dynamic Computation:** PyTorch uses a dynamic computational graph, making it more intuitive for debugging and dynamic model construction compared to static graph frameworks like TensorFlow 1.x.

- **Numpy Integration:** PyTorch seamlessly integrates with NumPy, making it easy to convert between NumPy arrays and PyTorch tensors.

- **Community and Research Focus:** PyTorch is favored by many researchers for its simplicity and flexibility, making it a prominent choice in academia.

- **TorchScript:** PyTorch offers TorchScript, a Just-in-Time (JIT) compiler that allows you to export models for deployment in production environments.

9.3.3 Choosing Between TensorFlow and PyTorch

The choice between TensorFlow and PyTorch often depends on your specific needs and preferences:

- **TensorFlow:** Opt for TensorFlow when you require scalability, production-ready features, or when you want to leverage pre-trained models from TensorFlow Hub. It's also an excellent choice for TensorFlow Serving in production deployments.

- **PyTorch:** Choose PyTorch if you value dynamic computation, an intuitive interface, and a strong presence in the research community. PyTorch is particularly popular for research projects, rapid prototyping, and academic work.

9.3.4 Getting Started with TensorFlow and PyTorch

To get started with TensorFlow and PyTorch, you'll need to install the respective libraries and familiarize yourself with their documentation:

- **TensorFlow Installation:** You can install TensorFlow using pip with the command **pip install tensorflow**.

- **PyTorch Installation:** PyTorch installation instructions can be found at pytorch.org.

Once installed, explore the official documentation, tutorials, and a variety of resources available online to gain proficiency in these frameworks.

9.3.5 Summary

In this section, we've introduced two of the most influential deep learning frameworks, TensorFlow and PyTorch. These frameworks have played a pivotal role in advancing the field of deep learning and have empowered researchers and practitioners to build cutting-edge machine learning models.

Your journey into deep learning will often involve a choice between these frameworks based on your specific project requirements and personal preferences. Both TensorFlow and PyTorch offer robust toolsets and vibrant communities, ensuring you have the resources you need to excel in the world of deep learning.

Practice Exercises for Chapter 9: Neural Networks and Deep Learning:

1. **Building a Simple Neural Network:**

    - Implement a feedforward neural network with one hidden layer from scratch using NumPy. Train the network on a synthetic dataset (e.g., XOR problem) and evaluate its performance.

    - Explore different activation functions such as sigmoid, ReLU, and tanh in the hidden layer of the neural network. Compare the convergence speed and accuracy of the model with different activation functions.

2. **Deep Learning Frameworks:**

- Create a basic neural network using TensorFlow or PyTorch to classify images in the MNIST dataset. Experiment with different network architectures (e.g., number of layers, hidden units) and training parameters (e.g., learning rate, batch size) to optimize model performance.

- Use pre-trained models such as VGG16 or ResNet50 from model zoos like TensorFlow Hub or PyTorch Hub for image classification tasks. Fine-tune the pre-trained models on a custom dataset and evaluate their performance.

3. **Advanced Neural Network Architectures:**

- Implement a convolutional neural network (CNN) using TensorFlow or PyTorch to classify images in the CIFAR-10 dataset. Experiment with different CNN architectures (e.g., number of convolutional layers, filter sizes) and regularization techniques (e.g., dropout, batch normalization) to improve classification accuracy.

- Explore recurrent neural networks (RNNs) or long short-term memory (LSTM) networks for sequence prediction tasks such as text generation or time series forecasting. Train the RNN/LSTM models on a dataset of sequential data and evaluate their predictive performance.

4. **Transfer Learning:**

- Fine-tune a pre-trained CNN model (e.g., VGG16, ResNet50) on a new dataset for a different image classification task. Freeze the convolutional layers of the pre-trained model and train only the fully connected layers on the new dataset. Evaluate the transfer learning performance compared to training from scratch.

5. **Deep Learning Applications:**

- Apply deep learning techniques to a real-world problem such as image recognition, natural language processing, or medical image analysis. Collect or obtain a dataset relevant to the problem domain and develop a deep learning model to solve the problem.

Chapter 10. Natural Language Processing (NLP)

Natural Language Processing (NLP): Basics of Text Processing

Natural Language Processing (NLP) is a branch of artificial intelligence focused on enabling computers to understand, interpret, and generate human language. Text processing is a foundational aspect of NLP, involving the transformation of raw text data into a format suitable for analysis and modeling.

10.1.1 Understanding Text Data

Text data can vary widely in structure, content, and language. Before applying NLP techniques, it's crucial to understand the characteristics of the text data being analyzed. Some common considerations include:

- **Language:** Identifying the language(s) present in the text data.

- **Text Format:** Recognizing the format of the text, whether it's structured (e.g., documents, emails) or unstructured (e.g., social media posts, comments).

- **Text Length:** Understanding the length of the documents or text samples, which can influence preprocessing and analysis techniques.

Text Preprocessing

Text preprocessing involves several steps to clean and prepare raw text data for further analysis. Some key preprocessing steps include:

- **Tokenization:** Breaking down text into smaller units, such as words or tokens. Tokenization can be performed at different levels, including word-level, character-level, or subword-level.

- **Lowercasing:** Converting all text to lowercase to ensure consistency in text representation. This prevents the model from treating the same word with different capitalizations as distinct entities.

- **Removing Punctuation:** Eliminating punctuation marks, symbols, and special characters from the text. Punctuation typically does not carry significant semantic meaning and can be safely removed.

- **Removing Stop Words:** Stop words are common words that often occur frequently but carry little semantic value (e.g., "the", "is", "and"). Removing stop words helps reduce the dimensionality of the text data and improve computational efficiency.

- **Stemming and Lemmatization:** Stemming and lemmatization are techniques used to reduce words to their base or root form. Stemming involves stripping suffixes from words to obtain their root forms (e.g., "running" to "run"), while lemmatization uses vocabulary and morphological analysis to return a word to its lemma or dictionary form.

Natural Language Processing (NLP) is a specialized field within machine learning that focuses on the interaction between computers and human languages. In this section, we will explore the basics of text processing and delve into two common applications of NLP: sentiment analysis and text classification.

Tokenization:

Tokenization is the process of breaking down a text into individual units, or tokens. These units can be words, phrases, or even characters.

```
from nltk.tokenize import word_tokenize


text = "Natural Language Processing is fascinating!"
tokens = word_tokenize(text)
```

Lemmatization and Stemming:

Lemmatization and stemming are techniques used to reduce words to their base or root form.

```python
from nltk.stem import PorterStemmer, WordNetLemmatizer


# Stemming

stemmer = PorterStemmer()

stemmed_words = [stemmer.stem(word) for word in tokens]


# Lemmatization

lemmatizer = WordNetLemmatizer()

lemmatized_words = [lemmatizer.lemmatize(word) for word in tokens]


print("Stemmed words:", stemmed_words)

print("Lemmatized words:", lemmatized_words)
```

Stop Words:

Stop words are common words that are often removed during text processing as they usually don't carry much meaning.

```python
from nltk.corpus import stopwords


stop_words = set(stopwords.words('english'))

filtered_words = [word for word in tokens if word.lower() not in stop_words]

print("Filtered words:", filtered_words)
```

10.1.2 Text Representation

After preprocessing, text data needs to be represented in a numerical format that machine learning algorithms can process. Two common methods for text representation are:

Bag of Words (BoW)

The Bag of Words model represents each document as a vector of word counts. It creates a vocabulary from all unique words in the corpus, and each document's vector indicates the frequency of each word. While simple and effective, BoW does not consider word order or context, leading to a loss of sequential information.

TF-IDF (Term Frequency-Inverse Document Frequency)

TF-IDF calculates the importance of a word in a document relative to its frequency across all documents in the corpus. It assigns higher weights to words that are more specific to a document and less common across all documents. TF-IDF addresses some limitations of BoW by penalizing words that appear frequently across all documents, thus emphasizing the importance of rare words.

10.1.3 Text Processing Libraries

Several Python libraries simplify text processing tasks and provide implementations of common NLP techniques:

- **NLTK (Natural Language Toolkit):** NLTK is a comprehensive library for NLP tasks, offering functionalities for tokenization, stemming, lemmatization, part-of-speech tagging, named entity recognition, and more. It's widely used for educational purposes and research in NLP.

- **spaCy:** spaCy is a modern and efficient NLP library designed for production use. It provides pre-trained models for tokenization, named entity recognition, dependency parsing, and other NLP tasks. spaCy's pipeline architecture and efficient processing make it suitable for building scalable NLP applications.

- **scikit-learn:** While primarily a machine learning library, scikit-learn includes utilities for text preprocessing, feature extraction, and text vectorization. It offers implementations of algorithms for

BoW, TF-IDF vectorization, and feature selection, making it a convenient choice for integrating text processing into machine learning pipelines.

Text Preprocessing with NLTK:

```python
import nltk
from nltk.corpus import stopwords
from nltk.tokenize import word_tokenize
from nltk.stem import PorterStemmer, WordNetLemmatizer
import string

# Sample text for preprocessing
text = "Natural language processing (NLP) is a subfield of artificial intelligence."

# Tokenization
tokens = word_tokenize(text)

# Lowercasing
tokens_lower = [token.lower() for token in tokens]

# Removing Punctuation
tokens_no_punct = [token for token in tokens_lower if token not in string.punctuation]

# Removing Stop Words
stop_words = set(stopwords.words('english'))
```

```python
tokens_no_stop = [token for token in tokens_no_punct if token not in
stop_words]


# Stemming

stemmer = PorterStemmer()

stemmed_tokens = [stemmer.stem(token) for token in tokens_no_stop]


# Lemmatization

lemmatizer = WordNetLemmatizer()

lemmatized_tokens = [lemmatizer.lemmatize(token) for token in
tokens_no_stop]


print("Original Text:", text)

print("Tokenization:", tokens)

print("Lowercasing:", tokens_lower)

print("Without Punctuation:", tokens_no_punct)

print("Without Stop Words:", tokens_no_stop)

print("Stemming:", stemmed_tokens)

print("Lemmatization:", lemmatized_tokens)
```

Text Representation with scikit-learn (Bag of Words and TF-IDF):

```python
from sklearn.feature_extraction.text import CountVectorizer,
TfidfVectorizer


# Sample documents

documents = [
```

```python
    "This is the first document.",

    "This document is the second document.",

    "And this is the third one.",

    "Is this the first document?",

]


# Bag of Words (BoW) representation

bow_vectorizer = CountVectorizer()

bow_matrix = bow_vectorizer.fit_transform(documents)

print("Bag of Words Matrix:")

print(bow_matrix.toarray())

print("Vocabulary:", bow_vectorizer.get_feature_names())


# TF-IDF representation

tfidf_vectorizer = TfidfVectorizer()

tfidf_matrix = tfidf_vectorizer.fit_transform(documents)

print("\nTF-IDF Matrix:")

print(tfidf_matrix.toarray())

print("Vocabulary:", tfidf_vectorizer.get_feature_names())
```

These code examples demonstrate basic text preprocessing techniques using NLTK and text representation methods using scikit-learn's CountVectorizer (Bag of Words) and TfidfVectorizer (TF-IDF). You can run these examples in a Python environment to observe the preprocessing steps and the resulting text representations.

Text processing is a fundamental aspect of Natural Language Processing, enabling computers to understand and analyze human language. By preprocessing text data and representing it in a numerical format, we can extract meaningful insights and build models that effectively interpret and generate text. In the next section, we'll explore advanced NLP techniques such as sentiment analysis, text classification, named entity recognition, and more.

10.2 Sentiment Analysis and Text Classification

Sentiment Analysis:

Sentiment analysis and text classification are essential tasks in Natural Language Processing (NLP) that involve analyzing text data to determine sentiment, opinions, or categorization of text into predefined classes. In this section, we'll explore these tasks and techniques for performing sentiment analysis and text classification using Python.

Sentiment analysis, also known as opinion mining, is the process of identifying and extracting sentiment or subjective information from text data. It aims to determine the emotional tone or polarity of a piece of text, such as positive, negative, or neutral.

Approaches to Sentiment Analysis:

- **Rule-Based Sentiment Analysis:** Rule-based approaches use predefined rules and patterns to classify text sentiment. These rules may involve sentiment lexicons, grammatical patterns, or syntactic structures.

- **Machine Learning-Based Sentiment Analysis:** Machine learning models, such as Naive Bayes, Support Vector Machines (SVM), or Recurrent Neural Networks (RNNs), are trained on labeled datasets to classify text sentiment. These models learn to recognize patterns and features indicative of specific sentiment classes.

Example: Sentiment Analysis with NLTK

```
import nltk
```

```python
from nltk.sentiment import SentimentIntensityAnalyzer

# Sample text for sentiment analysis
text = "This movie is fantastic! I loved every minute of it."

# Initialize SentimentIntensityAnalyzer
sia = SentimentIntensityAnalyzer()

# Perform sentiment analysis
sentiment_score = sia.polarity_scores(text)

# Interpret sentiment score
if sentiment_score['compound'] > 0.5:
    sentiment = "Positive"
elif sentiment_score['compound'] < -0.5:
    sentiment = "Negative"
else:
    sentiment = "Neutral"

print("Text:", text)
print("Sentiment:", sentiment)
print("Sentiment Score:", sentiment_score)
```

Example: Sentiment Analysis Using TextBlob

```python
from textblob import TextBlob


# Example sentence

sentence = "I love this product! It's amazing."


# Analyzing sentiment

blob = TextBlob(sentence)

sentiment_score = blob.sentiment.polarity


if sentiment_score > 0:

    sentiment_label = "Positive"

elif sentiment_score < 0:

    sentiment_label = "Negative"

else:

    sentiment_label = "Neutral"


print(f"Sentiment: {sentiment_label} (Score: {sentiment_score})")
```

10.2.1 Text Classification

Text classification is the task of assigning predefined categories or labels to text documents based on their content. It is commonly used for tasks such as topic categorization, spam detection, sentiment analysis, and more.

Approaches to Text Classification:

- **Machine Learning-Based Text Classification:** Machine learning algorithms, including Logistic Regression, Naive Bayes, Decision Trees, and Neural Networks, are trained on labeled text data to classify documents into predefined categories.

- **Deep Learning-Based Text Classification:** Deep learning models, such as Convolutional Neural Networks (CNNs) or Recurrent Neural Networks (RNNs), are capable of learning hierarchical representations of text data and capturing complex patterns for accurate classification.

Example: Text Classification with scikit-learn

```python
from sklearn.datasets import fetch_20newsgroups
from sklearn.feature_extraction.text import TfidfVectorizer
from sklearn.model_selection import train_test_split
from sklearn.naive_bayes import MultinomialNB
from sklearn.metrics import classification_report


# Load sample dataset (20 newsgroups)
data = fetch_20newsgroups(subset='all', categories=['sci.space',
'comp.graphics'])


# Split data into train and test sets
X_train, X_test, y_train, y_test = train_test_split(data.data, data.target,
test_size=0.2, random_state=42)


# Vectorize text data using TF-IDF
vectorizer = TfidfVectorizer()
X_train_vect = vectorizer.fit_transform(X_train)
X_test_vect = vectorizer.transform(X_test)


# Train a Multinomial Naive Bayes classifier
classifier = MultinomialNB()
```

```
classifier.fit(X_train_vect, y_train)


# Evaluate the classifier

y_pred = classifier.predict(X_test_vect)

print("Classification Report:")

print(classification_report(y_test, y_pred,
target_names=data.target_names))
```

Example 2:

```
from sklearn.model_selection import train_test_split

from sklearn.feature_extraction.text import CountVectorizer

from sklearn.naive_bayes import MultinomialNB

from sklearn.metrics import accuracy_score, classification_report


# Example dataset

data = [("I love this product! It's amazing.", "Positive"),

    ("The quality is disappointing.", "Negative"),

    ("Neutral statement about a product.", "Neutral")]


# Splitting the dataset

X, y = zip(*data)

X_train, X_test, y_train, y_test = train_test_split(X, y, test_size=0.2,
random_state=42)


# Text vectorization

vectorizer = CountVectorizer()
```

```python
X_train_vectorized = vectorizer.fit_transform(X_train)
X_test_vectorized = vectorizer.transform(X_test)


# Naive Bayes classifier
classifier = MultinomialNB()
classifier.fit(X_train_vectorized, y_train)


# Making predictions
predictions = classifier.predict(X_test_vectorized)


# Evaluating the model
accuracy = accuracy_score(y_test, predictions)
report = classification_report(y_test, predictions)


print(f"Accuracy: {accuracy}")
print("Classification Report:\n", report)
```

Example 3: Text Classification with BERT (Bidirectional Encoder
Representations from Transformers)

```python
from transformers import BertTokenizer,
TFBertForSequenceClassification
import tensorflow as tf


# Load pre-trained BERT tokenizer and model
tokenizer = BertTokenizer.from_pretrained('bert-base-uncased')
```

```
model = TFBertForSequenceClassification.from_pretrained('bert-base-
uncased')


# Tokenize and encode text data

inputs = tokenizer(texts, padding=True, truncation=True, max_length=128,
return_tensors='tf')


# Perform text classification

outputs = model(inputs)
```

Sentiment analysis and text classification are indispensable tools in natural language processing (NLP), offering profound insights into human emotions, opinions, and categorization of text data. These powerful techniques allow for the analysis of customer reviews, social media sentiment, or news articles, providing valuable insights into the underlying sentiment and themes present within text. Leveraging both traditional and deep learning methodologies, these tasks enable businesses and researchers to extract actionable insights from vast amounts of textual data. In the next section, we'll explore more advanced NLP tasks and techniques, such as named entity recognition, text summarization, and machine translation, unveiling the diverse capabilities and applications of natural language processing.

These examples showcase the fundamental techniques in NLP, including text processing, sentiment analysis, and text classification. As you delve deeper into NLP, you can explore more advanced techniques, such as named entity recognition, part-of-speech tagging, and sequence modeling, to tackle a wide range of language understanding tasks.

Practice Exercises for Chapter 10 on Natural Language Processing (NLP), focusing on sentiment analysis and text classification:

1. **Sentiment Analysis:**

- Perform sentiment analysis on a collection of movie reviews using a pre-trained sentiment analysis model like VADER or TextBlob. Evaluate the accuracy of the sentiment predictions.

- Implement a rule-based sentiment analysis system that assigns positive, negative, or neutral sentiment to text based on predefined rules and patterns. Test the system on various text samples and analyze its performance.

2. **Text Classification:**

- Build a text classifier to categorize news articles into different topics (e.g., sports, politics, technology) using a machine learning algorithm like Naive Bayes or SVM. Evaluate the classifier's performance using appropriate metrics such as accuracy, precision, recall, and F1 score.

- Explore deep learning-based text classification by fine-tuning a pre-trained language model (e.g., BERT, RoBERTa) on a text classification dataset such as the IMDb movie reviews dataset. Compare the performance of the fine-tuned model with traditional machine learning classifiers.

3. **Advanced NLP Techniques:**

- Implement a multi-class text classification system capable of detecting sentiment polarity (positive, negative, neutral) and emotion (e.g., happy, sad, angry) in text data.

- Experiment with ensemble methods for text classification, such as bagging or boosting, to improve classification accuracy. Compare the performance of the ensemble model with individual classifiers.

4. **Real-World Applications:**

- Design and develop a sentiment analysis tool for analyzing customer feedback on a product or service. Gather real-world data from online review platforms and evaluate the tool's performance.

- Create a text classification system for identifying fake news articles. Train the classifier on a dataset of labeled news articles and assess its ability to distinguish between real and fake news.

5. **Model Interpretability:**

   - Explore techniques for interpreting the predictions of a text classification model, such as feature importance analysis or visualization of attention weights in deep learning models. Investigate which words or phrases contribute most to the classification decision.

Chapter 11. Model Deployment

Model deployment is a crucial step in the machine learning pipeline, where a trained model is taken from a development environment and made available for making predictions on new, unseen data. In this section, we will explore the process of exporting and deploying models, along with integration into web applications.

11.1.1 Exporting and Deploying Models

Exporting Models:

Once a machine learning model is trained and optimized, it needs to be exported into a format suitable for deployment. This often involves saving the model weights, architecture, and any preprocessing steps.

```
# Example using TensorFlow

model.save('path_to_save_model')


# Example using PyTorch

torch.save(model.state_dict(), 'path_to_save_model.pth')
```

11.1.2 Exporting Trained Models

Exporting a trained model involves serializing its parameters and architecture to a file format that can be easily stored and loaded for inference. Several serialization formats are commonly used in the machine learning community, each with its advantages and suitability for different types of models.

Serialization Formats:

JSON (JavaScript Object Notation): JSON is a lightweight data interchange format that is human-readable and easy to parse. It's suitable for simple models or models with a small number of parameters.

Protocol Buffers (protobuf): Protobuf is a binary serialization format developed by Google that offers efficient data storage and transmission. It's often used for large-scale models or models trained on distributed systems.

HDF5 (Hierarchical Data Format): HDF5 is a file format designed to store and organize large amounts of data. It's commonly used for saving deep learning models trained with frameworks like TensorFlow or PyTorch.

Example: Exporting a Trained Model in TensorFlow

```python
import tensorflow as tf

# Assuming 'model' is a trained TensorFlow model
model.save('model.h5')  # Save model in HDF5 format
```

11.2 Model Deployment

Deploying a trained model involves setting up an infrastructure that can handle incoming data, pass it through the model, and return predictions in real-time. There are several deployment options available, each with its advantages and considerations.

Deployment Options:

- **API-Based Deployment:** Expose the model as a RESTful API endpoint, allowing clients to send HTTP requests with input data and receive predictions as responses. APIs offer flexibility and can be easily integrated into existing applications.

- **Containerization:** Package the model along with its dependencies into a container image using technologies like Docker. Containerization provides portability and ensures consistency across different environments.

- **Serverless Deployment:** Deploy the model as a serverless function on cloud platforms such as AWS Lambda or Google Cloud Functions. Serverless architectures offer automatic scaling and reduced operational overhead, making them ideal for low-latency applications with unpredictable traffic patterns.

Example: Deploying a Model as a RESTful API with Flask

```
from flask import Flask, request, jsonify

import joblib


app = Flask(__name__)


# Load the trained model

model = joblib.load('trained_model.pkl')


@app.route('/predict', methods=['POST'])

def predict():

    data = request.get_json()

    prediction = model.predict(data['features'])

    return jsonify({'prediction': prediction.tolist()})


if __name__ == '__main__':
```

```
app.run(debug=True)
```

Deployment Platforms:

Models can be deployed on various platforms, including cloud services like AWS, Azure, or Google Cloud, as well as edge devices or on-premises servers.

- **Cloud Deployment:**
    - Deploying models on cloud platforms allows for scalability and accessibility.
    - Platforms like TensorFlow Serving, SageMaker, or Azure ML provide dedicated environments for deploying and managing models.

- **Edge Deployment:**
    - Deploying models on edge devices is suitable for scenarios where low-latency and real-time processing are essential.
    - TensorFlow Lite, ONNX Runtime, or EdgeML are frameworks designed for edge deployment.

Model deployment is a crucial and critical step in the machine learning pipeline, essential for operationalizing machine learning models and enabling organizations to leverage their trained models for making predictions in real-world applications. This process involves exporting trained models and deploying them for inference in production environments, utilizing various deployment options such as APIs, containers, or serverless functions. In this section, we'll delve deeper into the intricacies of model deployment, exploring how organizations can unlock the full potential of their machine learning investments and drive innovation across industries by effectively deploying models in operational settings.

11.3 Integration with Web Applications

Integration with web applications is a pivotal aspect of deploying machine learning models, facilitating their seamless incorporation into user-facing interfaces such as websites or mobile apps. In this section, we'll delve deeper into various approaches and considerations for integrating deployed models with web applications.

1. RESTful APIs

RESTful APIs serve as a standard method for communication between web services and clients, enabling straightforward interaction with machine learning models over HTTP. Integrating a machine learning model into a web application via a RESTful API offers flexibility, scalability, and ease of integration across different platforms.

Implementation Steps:

1. **API Design:** Design clear and intuitive endpoints that encapsulate the model's functionality and expected input/output formats.

2. **Model Deployment:** Deploy the machine learning model as a RESTful API endpoint using frameworks like Flask, FastAPI, or Django REST Framework.

3. **Client Integration:** Incorporate API calls into the web application frontend or backend to send input data and process model predictions seamlessly.

2. JavaScript Integration

JavaScript libraries and frameworks empower web developers to execute machine learning models directly within the web browser, allowing for low-latency predictions and enhanced user experiences. This approach is particularly useful for applications requiring client-side inference or offline capabilities.

Implementation Steps:

1. **Model Conversion:** Convert trained machine learning models to formats compatible with JavaScript, such as TensorFlow.js or ONNX.js.

2. **Client-Side Deployment:** Serve the converted model files through a web server or content delivery network (CDN) for efficient access.

3. **Client Integration:** Incorporate model loading and inference logic into the web application using JavaScript libraries like TensorFlow.js or WebAssembly, enabling client-side prediction capabilities.

3. Server-Side Integration

For computationally intensive models or those requiring access to extensive datasets, server-side integration may be more appropriate. In this approach, the web application backend communicates with the deployed machine learning model on the server to generate predictions.

Implementation Steps:

1. **Model Deployment:** Deploy the machine learning model on the server using frameworks like Flask, Django, or Node.js, ensuring scalability and robustness.

2. **API Integration:** Expose the model's functionality through API endpoints that the web application backend can access securely.

3. **Backend Integration:** Integrate API requests and responses into the web application backend to perform inference and process predictions efficiently, maintaining a smooth user experience.

4. Real-Time Updates and Feedback

To enhance user engagement and model performance, implementing mechanisms for real-time updates and feedback between the web application and the deployed model is paramount. These mechanisms enable continuous improvement and refinement of the model based on user interactions and feedback.

Implementation Steps:

1. **Real-Time Communication:** Utilize web socket connections or server-sent events (SSE) to establish bi-directional communication channels between the web application and the model server, ensuring real-time updates and responsiveness.

2. **Feedback Mechanisms:** Enable users to provide feedback on model predictions directly within the web application, facilitating iterative model improvement and adaptation to evolving user needs and preferences.

Creating APIs:

To integrate machine learning models into web applications, you often expose them through APIs (Application Programming Interfaces). APIs allow web applications to communicate with the deployed models and receive predictions.

```python
# Example using Flask for creating a simple API
from flask import Flask, request, jsonify

app = Flask(__name__)

@app.route('/predict', methods=['POST'])
def predict():
    data = request.get_json()
    # Process input data and make predictions
    predictions = model.predict(data['input'])
    return jsonify(predictions.tolist())

if __name__ == '__main__':
    app.run(port=5000)
```

Using JavaScript for Front-End Integration:

Web applications, particularly those built with JavaScript frameworks like React or Vue.js, can easily integrate with machine learning models by making API requests.

```javascript
// Example using JavaScript (Axios library)
```

```
const inputData = { input: [1, 2, 3, 4, 5] };

axios.post('http://localhost:5000/predict', inputData)
  .then(response => {
    const predictions = response.data;
    // Process predictions in the front end
  })
  .catch(error => {
    console.error('Error making API request:', error);
  });
```

Server-Side Integration with Flask (RESTful API)

Flask is used to create a RESTful API that exposes an endpoint for model prediction. The client (web application) sends a POST request with input data to the **/predict** endpoint, and the server responds with the model's prediction.

```
# app.py
from flask import Flask, request, jsonify
import joblib

app = Flask(__name__)

# Load the pre-trained machine learning model
model = joblib.load('path/to/your/model.pkl')

@app.route('/predict', methods=['POST'])
```

```python
def predict():

    data = request.get_json()

    features = data['features']

    prediction = model.predict([features])[0]

    return jsonify({'prediction': prediction})


if __name__ == '__main__':

    app.run(debug=True)
```

Client-Side Integration with TensorFlow.js

TensorFlow.js is used to load a pre-trained model directly in the web browser. The model is loaded asynchronously, and the client can input data through a text field. Upon clicking the "Predict" button, the model makes a prediction based on the input data, and the result is displayed on the web page.

```html
<!-- index.html -->

<!DOCTYPE html>

<html>

<head>

    <title>Machine Learning Model Demo</title>

    <script
src="https://cdn.jsdelivr.net/npm/@tensorflow/tfjs@3.0.0"></script>

</head>

<body>

    <h1>Machine Learning Model Demo</h1>

    <label for="input">Input:</label>

    <input type="text" id="input">
```

```html
<button onclick="predict()">Predict</button>
<p id="output"></p>

<script>
    async function predict() {
        const input = document.getElementById('input').value;
        const model = await tf.loadLayersModel('path/to/your/model.json');
        const prediction = model.predict(tf.tensor([input]));
        const output = document.getElementById('output');
        output.innerText = 'Prediction: ' + prediction.dataSync()[0];
    }
</script>
</body>
</html>
```

Deploying Models with Cloud Services:

Major cloud providers offer services for deploying machine learning models seamlessly. For example, Google Cloud AI Platform, AWS Sagemaker, and Azure ML enable easy deployment and integration into web applications.

By following these steps, you can seamlessly integrate your machine learning models into web applications, making predictions accessible to end-users. Whether deployed on the cloud, edge devices, or on-premises servers, the goal is to provide a reliable and scalable prediction service for your models.

Practice Exercises for Chapter 11

1. **API Implementation:**

   - Design and implement a RESTful API endpoint using Flask or FastAPI to deploy a pre-trained machine learning model for sentiment analysis. The API should accept text input and return the predicted sentiment (positive, negative, neutral) as JSON response.

2. **Containerization:**

   - Create a Dockerfile to containerize a machine learning model along with its dependencies. Build and run the Docker container locally, and verify that the model can be accessed and used for inference.

3. **Serverless Deployment:**

   - Deploy a pre-trained image classification model as a serverless function on a cloud platform like AWS Lambda or Google Cloud Functions. Set up an HTTP trigger to invoke the function and test its ability to classify images sent in the request payload.

4. **Scaling Considerations:**

   - Explore strategies for scaling a deployed machine learning model to handle increased traffic and workload. Discuss options such as horizontal scaling (adding more instances) vs. vertical scaling (upgrading instance size), and their implications on performance and cost.

5. **Monitoring and Logging:**

   - Implement logging and monitoring mechanisms for a deployed model to track performance metrics such as inference latency, throughput, and error rates. Use tools like Prometheus and Grafana to visualize and analyze the collected data.

6. **Security and Authentication:**

   - Enhance the security of a deployed model by implementing authentication and authorization mechanisms. Explore options such as API keys, OAuth tokens, or JWT (JSON Web Tokens) for controlling access to the model API.

7. **Model Versioning:**

   - Develop a system for managing multiple versions of a deployed machine learning model to support A/B testing, gradual rollout, and rollback of model updates. Discuss strategies for maintaining backward compatibility and handling data drift.

8. **Continuous Integration/Continuous Deployment (CI/CD):**

   - Set up a CI/CD pipeline to automate the deployment of machine learning models from development to production environments. Use tools like Jenkins, GitLab CI, or GitHub Actions to orchestrate the pipeline and ensure smooth deployment process.

9. **Cost Optimization:**

   - Analyze the cost implications of deploying and serving machine learning models in different deployment scenarios (e.g., API-based, containerized, serverless). Identify cost-saving opportunities such as resource optimization, auto-scaling, and spot instances.

10. **Regulatory Compliance:**

    - Ensure compliance with regulatory requirements (e.g., GDPR, HIPAA) when deploying machine learning models that handle sensitive data. Implement privacy-preserving techniques such as data anonymization, encryption, and access controls to protect user privacy.

Chapter 12. Reinforcement Learning

Reinforcement learning is a paradigm in machine learning where an agent learns to make decisions by interacting with an environment and receiving feedback in the form of rewards or penalties. In this section, we will explore the basics of reinforcement learning, introduce Q-learning as a fundamental algorithm, and touch upon deep reinforcement learning, a more advanced approach that leverages neural networks.

12. Reinforcement Learning

Reinforcement Learning (RL) is a dynamic field of machine learning concerned with how agents learn to make sequential decisions by interacting with an environment to achieve long-term goals. It draws inspiration from behavioral psychology, where learning is driven by rewards and punishments.

Key Concepts:

1. **Agent-Environment Interaction:** At each time step, the agent observes the environment's state, selects an action, and receives a reward and the next state.

2. **Rewards and Cumulative Returns:** The agent's goal is to maximize cumulative rewards over time. Rewards serve as immediate feedback on the goodness of actions.

3. **Exploration and Exploitation:** RL agents face the exploration-exploitation dilemma, where they must balance exploring new actions to learn and exploiting known actions to maximize rewards.

4. **Policy:** A policy is a mapping from states to actions, defining the agent's behavior. It can be deterministic or stochastic.

5. **Value Function:** The value function estimates the expected return from being in a particular state and following a particular policy.

6. **Q-Learning and SARSA:** Classic RL algorithms like Q-learning and SARSA estimate the value of state-action pairs and update their estimates based on experienced rewards.

7. **Deep Reinforcement Learning (DRL):** DRL combines RL with deep neural networks, enabling agents to learn directly from raw sensory inputs, such as images or text.

8. **Markov Decision Processes (MDPs):** RL problems are often formalized as MDPs, consisting of states, actions, transition probabilities, and rewards.

Basic Reinforcement Learning Workflow:

1. **Initialization:** Initialize the environment, agent, and parameters.

2. **Action Selection:** The agent selects actions based on its policy, exploration strategy, or value estimates.

3. **Observation and Reward:** The agent observes the environment's state and receives a reward.

4. **Learning:** The agent updates its policy or value function based on observed states, actions, rewards, and transitions.

5. **Evaluation:** Assess the learned policy's performance through simulation or interaction with the real environment.

6. **Iteration:** Repeat the process, gradually improving the agent's policy or value function.

Applications:

1. **Game Playing:** RL has achieved remarkable success in mastering complex games like Chess, Go, and video games.

2. **Robotics:** RL enables robots to learn control policies for locomotion, manipulation, and navigation in real-world environments.

3. **Autonomous Vehicles:** RL techniques are used to train self-driving cars to make decisions in complex traffic scenarios.

4. **Recommendation Systems:** RL can optimize recommendation algorithms by learning user preferences and delivering personalized content.

5. **Finance:** RL algorithms are employed in algorithmic trading, portfolio optimization, and risk management in financial markets.

Challenges:

1. **Sample Efficiency:** RL algorithms often require a large number of interactions with the environment to learn effective policies.

2. **Generalization:** Agents must generalize learned policies across different states and environments to perform well in unseen situations.

3. **Exploration-Exploitation Tradeoff:** Balancing between exploring new actions to discover better strategies and exploiting known actions to maximize rewards.

4. **Reward Design:** Designing appropriate reward functions that incentivize desirable behaviors and discourage undesirable ones.

Reinforcement Learning offers a powerful framework for training intelligent agents to make decisions in uncertain and complex environments. By understanding its fundamental concepts, workflow, applications, and challenges, practitioners can apply RL techniques to solve a wide range of real-world problems, from robotics and autonomous systems to finance and healthcare.

Basics of Reinforcement Learning

Key Components:

Reinforcement learning involves three main components: the agent, the environment, and the rewards.

- **Agent:**

    - The entity making decisions and taking actions within the environment.

- **Environment:**

    - The external system with which the agent interacts.

- **Rewards:**

    - Feedback provided to the agent based on its actions, guiding it toward desired outcomes.

Exploration vs. Exploitation:

An essential challenge in reinforcement learning is the exploration-exploitation trade-off. The agent must balance exploring new actions to discover their effects and exploiting known actions to maximize cumulative rewards.

Q-learning and Deep Reinforcement Learning

Q-learning:

Q-learning is a fundamental reinforcement learning algorithm used for solving Markov Decision Processes (MDPs) without requiring a model of the environment. In Q-learning, an agent learns to estimate the value of taking a particular action in a specific state by updating a Q-table based on observed rewards and transitions. The Q-value represents the expected cumulative reward of taking an action in a state and following a particular policy thereafter.

The Q-learning algorithm iteratively updates Q-values using the Bellman equation:

$$Q(s, a) \leftarrow (1 - \alpha) \cdot Q(s, a) + \alpha \cdot (r + \gamma \cdot \max_{a'} Q(s', a'))$$

where:

- $Q(s,a)$ is the Q-value for state s and action a.

- r is the reward received after taking action a in state s.

- s' is the next state after taking action a.

- a is the learning rate, determining the weight of new information.

- γ is the discount factor, representing the importance of future rewards.

Q-learning is a model-free algorithm, meaning it does not require knowledge of the transition probabilities between states. It is often used for discrete state and action spaces, such as grid-world environments.

Deep Reinforcement Learning (DRL):

Deep Reinforcement Learning (DRL) combines reinforcement learning with deep neural networks to learn directly from high-dimensional sensory inputs, such as images or raw sensor data. DRL algorithms, such as Deep Q-Networks (DQN), enable agents to automatically discover complex patterns and representations from raw data, allowing them to solve more challenging tasks than traditional RL methods.

In DRL, a deep neural network is used to approximate the Q-value function. The network takes the state as input and outputs Q-values for all possible actions. The network is trained using a variant of Q-learning, where the loss function is defined as the Mean Squared Error (MSE) between the predicted Q-values and the target Q-values obtained from the Bellman equation.

DRL has achieved significant success in a variety of domains, including playing video games, controlling robots, and autonomous driving. However, training deep RL agents can be challenging due to issues such as sample inefficiency, exploration-exploitation trade-offs, and unstable training dynamics.

Key Differences:

1. **Representation:** Q-learning uses a tabular representation (Q-table) to store Q-values for all state-action pairs, while DRL employs deep neural networks to approximate the Q-value function.

2. **Scalability:** DRL can handle high-dimensional state spaces and continuous action spaces more effectively than Q-learning, making it suitable for complex real-world problems.

3. **Sample Efficiency:** Q-learning is generally more sample-efficient than DRL because it updates Q-values based on individual transitions, whereas DRL often requires large amounts of data to train deep neural networks effectively.

In summary, Q-learning is a foundational RL algorithm suitable for discrete action spaces, while DRL extends RL to handle high-dimensional input spaces and continuous action spaces by leveraging deep neural networks. Both approaches have their strengths and limitations, and the choice between them depends on the specific characteristics of the problem at hand.

12.2 Q-learning

Q-learning Algorithm:

Q-learning is a model-free reinforcement learning algorithm that aims to find an optimal policy for an agent in a Markov decision process (MDP).

- **Q-Values:**
  - Q-values represent the expected cumulative rewards for taking a specific action in a given state.

- **Q-Table:**
  - In simple environments, Q-values can be stored in a Q-table, where each entry corresponds to a state-action pair.

Q-learning pseudocode

```
Initialize Q-table with zeros
For each episode:
    Observe the current state (s)
    Choose an action (a) using an exploration-exploitation strategy
    Take the chosen action and observe the new state (s') and reward (r)
    Update Q-value for the chosen action using the Q-learning update rule
```

Below is a simple Python code example illustrating how to implement a basic Q-learning algorithm for solving the classic "Frozen Lake" environment from OpenAI Gym:

```
import numpy as np
```

```python
import gym

# Create the Frozen Lake environment
env = gym.make('FrozenLake-v1')

# Initialize Q-table with zeros
Q = np.zeros([env.observation_space.n, env.action_space.n])

# Set hyperparameters
learning_rate = 0.8
discount_factor = 0.95
num_episodes = 1000

# Q-learning algorithm
for episode in range(num_episodes):
    state = env.reset()
    done = False

    while not done:
        # Choose action using epsilon-greedy policy
        if np.random.rand() < 0.5:
            action = env.action_space.sample()  # Explore
        else:
            action = np.argmax(Q[state, :])  # Exploit
```

```
    # Perform action and observe new state and reward

    new_state, reward, done, _ = env.step(action)


    # Update Q-value using Bellman equation

    Q[state, action] += learning_rate * (reward + discount_factor *
np.max(Q[new_state, :]) - Q[state, action])


    # Transition to new state

    state = new_state


# Evaluate learned policy

total_rewards = 0

num_episodes = 100

for _ in range(num_episodes):

    state = env.reset()

    done = False


    while not done:

        action = np.argmax(Q[state, :])  # Greedy policy

        new_state, reward, done, _ = env.step(action)

        total_rewards += reward

        state = new_state


average_reward = total_rewards / num_episodes

print("Average reward over 100 episodes:", average_reward)
```

This code trains a Q-learning agent to navigate the Frozen Lake environment and then evaluates its performance by averaging rewards over 100 episodes. You can further extend this example by experimenting with different hyperparameters, modifying the environment, or implementing more complex RL algorithms such as Deep Q-Networks (DQN).

Deep Q-Network (DQN) implementation using Python and the OpenAI Gym library:

Deep Q-Network (DQN):

```python
import numpy as np

import tensorflow as tf

import gym


# Create the CartPole environment

env = gym.make('CartPole-v1')


# Define neural network architecture

model = tf.keras.Sequential([

    tf.keras.layers.Dense(64, activation='relu',
input_shape=(env.observation_space.shape[0],)),

    tf.keras.layers.Dense(64, activation='relu'),

    tf.keras.layers.Dense(env.action_space.n, activation='linear')

])


# Compile the model

model.compile(optimizer=tf.keras.optimizers.Adam(learning_rate=0.001),
```

```python
        loss='mse')


# Define hyperparameters
gamma = 0.99
epsilon = 1.0
epsilon_min = 0.01
epsilon_decay = 0.995
batch_size = 32
num_episodes = 1000


# Replay memory
replay_memory = []


# Deep Q-Network (DQN) algorithm
for episode in range(num_episodes):
    state = env.reset()
    state = np.reshape(state, [1, env.observation_space.shape[0]])
    done = False
    total_reward = 0

    while not done:
        # Epsilon-greedy action selection
        if np.random.rand() <= epsilon:
            action = env.action_space.sample()  # Explore
        else:
```

```python
        action = np.argmax(model.predict(state))  # Exploit


        # Take action and observe new state and reward
        next_state, reward, done, _ = env.step(action)
        next_state = np.reshape(next_state, [1,
env.observation_space.shape[0]])
        total_reward += reward


        # Store transition in replay memory
        replay_memory.append((state, action, reward, next_state, done))


        # Sample minibatch from replay memory
        minibatch = random.sample(replay_memory, batch_size)


        # Update Q-values using minibatch
        for s, a, r, s_, d in minibatch:
            target = r
            if not d:
                target = r + gamma * np.max(model.predict(s_)[0])
            target_f = model.predict(s)
            target_f[0][a] = target
            model.fit(s, target_f, epochs=1, verbose=0)


        # Update state
        state = next_state
```

```
    # Decay exploration rate
    if epsilon > epsilon_min:
        epsilon *= epsilon_decay


    # Print episode information
    print("Episode {}: Total Reward = {}".format(episode+1, total_reward))
```

These examples demonstrate basic Q-learning for a discrete action space (Frozen Lake environment) and Deep Q-Network (DQN) for a continuous action space (CartPole environment). You can further customize and extend these implementations for other RL problems and environments.

12.3 Deep Reinforcement Learning

Introduction to Deep Reinforcement Learning:

Deep reinforcement learning combines reinforcement learning with deep neural networks to handle high-dimensional state spaces.

- **Deep Q-Network (DQN):**
  - DQN is a model that approximates the Q-function using a deep neural network.

- **Experience Replay:**
  - To improve stability, DQN utilizes experience replay, storing past experiences and randomly sampling batches for training.

- **Target Networks:**
  - DQN employs two networks: the target network and the online network, to stabilize the learning process.

```
# DQN pseudocode
Initialize replay memory
```

```
Initialize target and online Q-networks with random weights

For each episode:

    Observe the current state (s)

    Choose an action (a) using an exploration-exploitation strategy

    Take the chosen action and observe the new state (s') and reward (r)

    Store the experience (s, a, r, s') in replay memory

    Sample a random batch from replay memory

    Update Q-values using the DQN loss function

    Update target network periodically
```

Deep reinforcement learning has achieved remarkable success in tasks such as playing games (e.g., AlphaGo, Atari games) and robotic control, showcasing its ability to handle complex environments.

Chapter 12 End-of-chapter practice problems

1. **Q-learning Practice Problem**: Implement Q-learning for solving the GridWorld environment in OpenAI Gym. Train an agent to navigate from the start state to the goal state while avoiding obstacles. Experiment with different hyperparameters such as learning rate and discount factor to observe their effects on learning performance.

2. **Policy Iteration Practice Problem**: Implement the Policy Iteration algorithm to solve the Taxi-v3 environment in OpenAI Gym. Evaluate the performance of the learned policy and compare it with the results obtained using value iteration. Analyze the convergence speed and computational efficiency of policy iteration.

3. **Model-Free Control Practice Problem**: Develop a Monte Carlo control algorithm to solve the Blackjack-v0 environment in OpenAI Gym. Train an agent to learn an optimal policy for playing blackjack. Compare the performance of on-policy and off-policy methods such as SARSA and Q-learning.

4. **Deep Q-Learning Practice Problem**: Implement a Deep Q-Network (DQN) to solve the LunarLander-v2 environment in OpenAI Gym. Train a neural network to learn a policy for landing a lunar module safely on the moon's surface. Experiment with different network architectures, loss functions, and optimization algorithms to improve learning stability and convergence.

5. **Multi-Agent Reinforcement Learning Practice Problem**: Design a multi-agent reinforcement learning system for solving the Multi-Agent Particle Environment (MAPE) in OpenAI Gym. Train multiple agents to collaborate or compete with each other to achieve a common goal or maximize individual rewards. Explore cooperative and competitive strategies to achieve optimal performance.

6. **Continuous Action Space Practice Problem**: Extend the DDPG (Deep Deterministic Policy Gradient) algorithm to solve the Pendulum-v0 environment in OpenAI Gym. Train an agent to learn a continuous control policy for swinging up and balancing a pendulum using deep neural networks. Experiment with different exploration strategies and action space representations to enhance learning stability and performance.

7. **Hierarchical Reinforcement Learning Practice Problem**: Implement a hierarchical reinforcement learning algorithm to solve the Taxi-v3 environment in OpenAI Gym. Learn a high-level policy for navigating between different locations and a low-level policy for performing actions within each location. Analyze the benefits of hierarchical decomposition in terms of learning efficiency and scalability.

8. **Real-World Application Practice Problem**: Choose a real-world application domain such as robotic manipulation, autonomous driving, or financial trading. Formulate a reinforcement learning problem statement and design an experimental setup using appropriate simulation environments or physical hardware. Implement and evaluate different RL algorithms to address the specified problem and analyze the practical implications of the results.

Chapter 13. Model Interpretability

Model interpretability is a critical aspect of machine learning, both in terms of enabling users to understand how models make predictions and allowing stakeholders to trust and validate these predictions. This section will delve into the importance of understanding and interpreting machine learning models, particularly in complex systems involving deep neural networks and ensemble methods, where deciphering the decision-making process can be challenging. We will explore techniques for assessing feature importance and obtaining model explanations, aiming to make the inner workings of models more transparent and understandable. These interpretability techniques help address the challenges of model comprehension, thereby enhancing the trust and reliability of machine learning systems.

Understanding Machine Learning Models:

1. **Feature Importance Analysis**:

    - Feature importance analysis techniques aim to identify the most influential features in a model's decision-making process. These techniques assign importance scores to individual features based on their contribution to the model's predictions.

    - Permutation importance, SHAP (SHapley Additive exPlanations), and LIME (Local Interpretable Model-agnostic Explanations) are commonly used methods for feature importance analysis. Permutation importance involves randomly shuffling the values of each feature and measuring the impact on model performance, while SHAP and LIME provide local explanations for individual predictions.

2. **Partial Dependence Plots (PDPs)**:

    - PDPs visualize the marginal effect of a feature on the predicted outcome while marginalizing over the values of other features. By plotting the predicted outcome against different values of a single feature while keeping other features constant, PDPs provide insights into the relationship between individual features and the model's predictions.

- PDPs are particularly useful for identifying nonlinear relationships between features and predictions and understanding how changes in feature values affect model outputs.

3. **Individual Conditional Expectation (ICE) Plots**:

- ICE plots extend PDPs by providing the predicted outcome for each instance in the dataset, allowing for a more granular analysis of feature effects. Instead of aggregating the effects of a feature across all instances, ICE plots show the effect of a feature on each individual instance.

- ICE plots are valuable for understanding heterogeneity in the effects of a feature across different data points and identifying potential interactions between features.

4. **Model-specific Interpretability Techniques**:

- Some models inherently offer interpretability due to their transparent structure. For example, decision trees and linear models are often considered interpretable models because their decision-making processes are easy to understand.

- Decision trees can be visualized to understand the decision paths and feature splits, providing insights into how the model partitions the feature space. Similarly, linear models provide coefficients that indicate the importance of each feature in predicting the target variable.

Challenges and Considerations:

1. **Trade-offs with Complexity**:

- Increasing model interpretability often comes at the cost of model complexity and predictive performance. Simple, interpretable models may not capture the intricacies of the underlying data as effectively as complex, black-box models.

- Practitioners need to strike a balance between model interpretability and predictive accuracy based on the specific requirements of the application domain. In some cases, sacrificing a small amount of accuracy for increased interpretability may be acceptable if it enhances stakeholders' trust in the model.

2. **Interpretability vs. Performance**:

- Highly interpretable models may not always achieve the same level of performance as complex, black-box models. Deep neural networks and ensemble methods, while powerful in terms of predictive accuracy, often lack transparency and are difficult to interpret.

- Understanding the trade-offs between interpretability and performance is crucial when selecting an appropriate model for a given task. Decision-makers must weigh the benefits of interpretability against the potential gains in predictive accuracy.

3. **Ethical and Regulatory Compliance**:

- Interpretability is increasingly important for ensuring compliance with ethical guidelines and regulatory requirements, especially in sensitive domains such as healthcare, finance, and criminal justice.

- Transparent models help mitigate the risks of bias, discrimination, and unintended consequences by enabling stakeholders to identify and address potential sources of unfairness or harm. Interpretability techniques can reveal underlying biases in the data or model architecture, allowing for corrective measures to be implemented.

Model interpretability is a multifaceted concept that encompasses various techniques and considerations for understanding and explaining machine learning models. By employing interpretability techniques such as feature importance analysis, partial dependence plots, and model-specific explanations, practitioners can gain valuable insights into model behavior, identify potential biases or errors, and facilitate informed decision-making in real-world applications. In an era of increasing reliance on machine learning systems, prioritizing interpretability is essential for building trust, ensuring accountability, and promoting ethical and responsible AI practices.

13.1 Understanding and Interpreting Machine Learning Models

Why Model Interpretability Matters:

Model interpretability is crucial for various reasons, including:

- **Trust and Accountability:**

    - Understanding model predictions builds trust in the system, especially in applications where decisions impact individuals or communities.

- **Debugging and Improvement:**

    - Interpretable models facilitate debugging and improvement by revealing how the model processes information and identifying areas for enhancement.

- **Regulatory Compliance:**

    - In regulated industries, interpretability is often required to ensure compliance with standards and regulations.

Below are code examples demonstrating some interpretability techniques:

```python
# Importing necessary libraries
import numpy as np
import pandas as pd
from sklearn.datasets import load_boston
```

```python
from sklearn.ensemble import RandomForestRegressor
import matplotlib.pyplot as plt
from sklearn.inspection import plot_partial_dependence
from sklearn.linear_model import LinearRegression
from sklearn.tree import DecisionTreeRegressor
from sklearn.inspection import permutation_importance

# Load Boston housing dataset
boston = load_boston()
X = pd.DataFrame(boston.data, columns=boston.feature_names)
y = boston.target

# Problem 1: Feature Importance Analysis

# Train a random forest regressor
rf = RandomForestRegressor(n_estimators=100, random_state=42)
rf.fit(X, y)

# Calculate feature importance
feature_importance = rf.feature_importances_
sorted_idx = np.argsort(feature_importance)

# Plot feature importance
plt.figure(figsize=(10, 6))
plt.barh(range(X.shape[1]), feature_importance[sorted_idx], align='center')
```

```python
plt.yticks(range(X.shape[1]), np.array(boston.feature_names)[sorted_idx])
plt.xlabel('Feature Importance')
plt.ylabel('Feature')
plt.title('Random Forest Feature Importance')
plt.show()


# Problem 2: Partial Dependence Plots (PDPs)

# Train a decision tree regressor
dt = DecisionTreeRegressor(random_state=42)
dt.fit(X, y)


# Plot partial dependence plots for two features
plt.figure(figsize=(12, 6))
plot_partial_dependence(dt, X, features=[0, 5],
feature_names=boston.feature_names)
plt.suptitle('Partial Dependence Plots')
plt.show()


# Problem 3: Individual Conditional Expectation (ICE) Plots

# Plot ICE plots for two features
plt.figure(figsize=(12, 6))
plot_partial_dependence(dt, X, features=[0, 5],
feature_names=boston.feature_names, kind='individual')
plt.suptitle('Individual Conditional Expectation (ICE) Plots')
```

```python
plt.show()


# Problem 4: Model-specific Interpretability Techniques


# Train a linear regression model
lr = LinearRegression()
lr.fit(X, y)


# Calculate coefficients
coefficients = lr.coef_


# Print coefficients for each feature
for feature, coef in zip(boston.feature_names, coefficients):
    print(f'{feature}: {coef}')


# Problem 5: Permutation Importance


# Calculate permutation importance
perm_importance = permutation_importance(rf, X, y, n_repeats=30,
random_state=42)


# Plot permutation importance
sorted_idx_perm = perm_importance.importances_mean.argsort()
plt.figure(figsize=(10, 6))
plt.barh(range(X.shape[1]),
perm_importance.importances_mean[sorted_idx_perm], align='center')
```

```
plt.yticks(range(X.shape[1]),
np.array(boston.feature_names)[sorted_idx_perm])

plt.xlabel('Permutation Importance')

plt.ylabel('Feature')

plt.title('Permutation Importance')

plt.show()
```

In this code block:

- Problem 1 demonstrates feature importance analysis using a random forest regressor.

- Problem 2 showcases partial dependence plots (PDPs) for two features using a decision tree regressor.

- Problem 3 displays individual conditional expectation (ICE) plots for the same features as in Problem 2.

- Problem 4 calculates and prints coefficients for each feature in a linear regression model.

- Problem 5 calculates permutation importance using a random forest regressor and visualizes the results.

13.2 Feature Importance and Model Explanations

Understanding the significance of features in a machine learning model and being able to elucidate its decisions are pivotal for model interpretability. Feature importance analysis aims to identify the most influential features, shedding light on the underlying data dynamics, while model explanations provide transparent justifications for individual predictions, bolstering the model's trustworthiness.

Feature Importance Analysis:

Feature importance analysis endeavors to quantify each feature's contribution to the model's predictive accuracy, allowing practitioners to glean insights into the data's underlying patterns. Several methods can be employed to ascertain feature importance:

1. **Permutation Importance**:

   - Permutation importance quantifies a feature's importance by measuring the reduction in model performance when the feature's values are randomly shuffled. A larger decrease in performance signifies higher feature importance.

   - This technique is versatile and can be applied to any machine learning model, providing a model-agnostic approach to feature assessment.

2. **SHAP Values (SHapley Additive exPlanations)**:

   - SHAP values offer a comprehensive framework for elucidating a model's output by attributing each feature's contribution to individual predictions.

   - Based on cooperative game theory principles, SHAP values provide a globally consistent measure of feature importance, facilitating a deeper understanding of model behavior.

3. **Feature Importance Plots**:

   - Feature importance plots visualize the relative importance of features in a graphical format, enabling practitioners to discern the most influential features at a glance.

   - While commonly employed for tree-based models like decision trees and random forests, these plots can be adapted for diverse algorithms, providing valuable insights into feature relevance.

Model Explanations:

While feature importance analysis offers insights at a global level, model explanations focus on providing interpretable justifications for individual predictions, crucial for building confidence in the model's decisions. Various techniques can be utilized for generating model explanations:

1. **Local Interpretable Model-agnostic Explanations (LIME)**:

   - LIME generates localized, human-interpretable explanations for individual predictions by approximating the model's behavior using interpretable surrogate models.

   - By perturbing the input data around the instance of interest and observing the resultant changes in predictions, LIME identifies the most influential features for that prediction, enhancing interpretability.

2. **Partial Dependence Plots (PDPs)**:

   - PDPs visualize the marginal effect of a feature on predictions while marginalizing over other feature values, offering insights into how predictions change with varying feature values.

   - These plots provide a holistic understanding of feature effects, enabling practitioners to discern relationships between features and predictions.

3. **Individual Conditional Expectation (ICE) Plots**:

   - ICE plots extend PDPs by providing the predicted outcome for each instance in the dataset, facilitating a more nuanced analysis of feature effects.

   - By plotting the predicted outcome for each instance against a specific feature's values, ICE plots highlight individual variations in feature effects, aiding in model interpretation.

- **Permutation Importance:**

  - Shuffling individual features and measuring the impact on model performance.

```python
from sklearn.inspection import permutation_importance


# Assuming model is your trained model, and X_test is your test data
```

```
perm_importance = permutation_importance(model, X_test, y_test)
```

Feature Importance from Tree-based Models:

- Decision tree-based models (e.g., Random Forests, Gradient Boosting) provide built-in feature importance scores.

-

```
# Example using a Random Forest model
importances = model.feature_importances_
```

In addition to feature importance, model explanations provide insights into individual predictions. Techniques for obtaining model explanations include:

- **LIME (Local Interpretable Model-agnostic Explanations):**
  - LIME creates local interpretable models around specific instances to approximate the behavior of the complex model.

```
from lime.lime_tabular import LimeTabularExplainer


explainer = LimeTabularExplainer(X_train.values, mode='classification')
explanation = explainer.explain_instance(X_test.iloc[0],
model.predict_proba)
```

SHAP (SHapley Additive exPlanations):

- SHAP values allocate contributions of each feature to the difference between the model's prediction and the average prediction.

```
import shap
```

```
explainer = shap.Explainer(model)
shap_values = explainer.shap_values(X_test)
```

These techniques allow practitioners to gain insights into model decisions, making machine learning more transparent and accountable. By understanding feature importance and obtaining model explanations, users can navigate the trade-off between model complexity and interpretability.

Feature importance analysis and model explanations play pivotal roles in enhancing model interpretability, fostering understanding, validation, and trust in machine learning models. By discerning influential features and providing transparent explanations for predictions, these techniques elevate the transparency, accountability, and reliability of machine learning systems in real-world scenarios.

Practice Problems for Chapter 13: Model Interpretability

1. **Understanding Model Predictions:**

   - Select a pre-trained classification model (e.g., logistic regression, random forest, neural network) and apply it to a dataset of your choice. Analyze a set of predictions made by the model and identify instances where the model's predictions are confident or uncertain. Investigate the feature values of these instances to understand the factors influencing the model's predictions.

2. **Feature Importance Analysis:**

   - Train a decision tree-based model (e.g., random forest, gradient boosting) on a dataset with a large number of features. Calculate the feature importance scores provided by the model and identify the top important features. Visualize the feature importance scores using a bar plot or a heatmap to gain insights into the relative importance of different features in the model's decision-making process.

3. **Model Explanation Techniques:**

- Apply SHAP (SHapley Additive exPlanations) or LIME (Local Interpretable Model-agnostic Explanations) to explain the predictions of a black-box model (e.g., support vector machine, deep neural network). Generate local explanations for individual predictions and visualize the contribution of each feature to the model's output. Compare the explanations provided by SHAP and LIME and analyze their consistency and interpretability.

4. **Permutation Importance Analysis:**

- Implement permutation importance analysis to evaluate the feature importance of a trained model. Randomly shuffle the values of each feature in the test set and measure the decrease in model performance (e.g., accuracy, F1-score) after shuffling. Rank the features based on their importance scores and compare them with the feature importance scores obtained from the model.

5. **Model Complexity Analysis:**

- Train a series of models with varying degrees of complexity (e.g., different depths for decision trees, different numbers of hidden units for neural networks) on a dataset. Evaluate the performance of each model on a validation set and analyze the trade-off between model complexity and performance. Determine the optimal level of model complexity that balances predictive accuracy and interpretability.

Chapter 14. Advanced Topics

In this section, we will explore advanced topics that enhance the capabilities of machine learning models, including transfer learning, AutoML (Automated Machine Learning), and hyperparameter tuning.

Transfer learning is a machine learning technique where a model trained on one task is reused or adapted as the starting point for a model on a second related task. This approach is particularly useful when the second task has limited labeled data or when the tasks share some underlying patterns or features. Transfer learning can significantly reduce the amount of labeled data required to train a new model and improve its performance, especially in domains where data is scarce or expensive to acquire.

How Transfer Learning Works:

In transfer learning, a pre-trained model, typically trained on a large dataset for a related task, serves as the starting point. Instead of training a new model from scratch, the pre-trained model's knowledge, usually represented in the form of learned weights, is transferred or fine-tuned to the new task. This allows the model to leverage the learned features, representations, or patterns from the source task, thereby accelerating the learning process and potentially improving performance on the target task.

14.1 Transfer Learning

Concept of Transfer Learning:

Transfer learning is a technique where a model trained on one task is leveraged for a different but related task. Instead of training a model from scratch, transfer learning uses the knowledge gained from one domain to improve performance in another.

Applications of Transfer Learning:

- **Image Classification:**
  - Pre-trained convolutional neural networks (CNNs) can be fine-tuned on a specific dataset for image classification tasks.

- **Natural Language Processing (NLP):**

- Pre-trained language models, such as BERT or GPT, can be adapted to specific NLP tasks like sentiment analysis or named entity recognition.

Implementation in TensorFlow (Example):

```python
from tensorflow import keras
from tensorflow.keras.applications import VGG16
from tensorflow.keras.layers import Dense, Flatten
from tensorflow.keras.models import Model


# Load pre-trained VGG16 model without the final fully connected layers
base_model = VGG16(weights='imagenet', include_top=False,
input_shape=(224, 224, 3))


# Add custom layers for the specific task
x = Flatten()(base_model.output)
x = Dense(256, activation='relu')(x)
output = Dense(num_classes, activation='softmax')(x)


# Create the transfer learning model
transfer_model = Model(inputs=base_model.input, outputs=output)


# Compile and train the model on the target task
transfer_model.compile(optimizer='adam', loss='categorical_crossentropy',
metrics=['accuracy'])
transfer_model.fit(train_data, epochs=10, validation_data=val_data)
```

Transfer Learning Approaches:

There are several approaches to transfer learning, including:

1. **Feature Extraction**: In this approach, the pre-trained model's learned features are extracted as fixed representations of the input data. These features are then used as input to train a new model specifically for the target task. Commonly used pre-trained models for feature extraction include convolutional neural networks (CNNs) pre-trained on large image datasets like ImageNet for computer vision tasks and pre-trained word embeddings like Word2Vec or GloVe for natural language processing tasks.

2. **Fine-tuning**: Fine-tuning involves further training the pre-trained model on the target task with the new labeled data, typically using a smaller learning rate to prevent drastic changes to the learned representations. By fine-tuning the model's parameters on the target task, it can adapt its learned features to better suit the specifics of the new task. Fine-tuning is especially effective when the source and target tasks are closely related, and the new task has enough labeled data to refine the pre-trained model's parameters effectively.

Benefits of Transfer Learning:

- **Reduced Training Time**: Transfer learning allows models to be trained faster since they start with pre-learned representations, thereby requiring fewer epochs of training.

- **Improved Generalization**: By leveraging knowledge from a related task, transfer learning often leads to models that generalize better to new, unseen data.

- **Effective Use of Limited Data**: Transfer learning enables the effective utilization of limited labeled data by leveraging knowledge from larger, pre-existing datasets.

Considerations and Best Practices:

- **Choice of Pre-trained Model**: Selecting an appropriate pre-trained model that is relevant to the target task is crucial for successful transfer learning.

- **Task Similarity**: The success of transfer learning depends on the similarity between the source and target tasks. Closer task alignment generally leads to better transfer performance.

- **Data Augmentation**: Complementing transfer learning with data augmentation techniques can further enhance the model's performance, especially when labeled data is limited.

- **Fine-tuning Strategy**: Carefully choose the layers to fine-tune and the learning rate schedule to prevent overfitting and instability during training.

Applications of Transfer Learning:

Transfer learning has been successfully applied across various domains, including computer vision, natural language processing, and healthcare. For instance, in computer vision, pre-trained CNNs like ResNet and VGGNet have been adapted for tasks such as image classification, object detection, and image segmentation. In natural language processing, pre-trained language models like BERT and GPT have been fine-tuned for tasks like sentiment analysis, named entity recognition, and machine translation.

Below are code examples demonstrating how to implement transfer learning using TensorFlow and Keras for fine-tuning a pre-trained convolutional neural network (CNN) on a new dataset:

```
import numpy as np

import tensorflow as tf

from tensorflow.keras.applications import VGG16

from tensorflow.keras.preprocessing.image import ImageDataGenerator

from tensorflow.keras import layers, models, optimizers


# Load pre-trained VGG16 model without top (fully connected) layers
```

```python
base_model = VGG16(weights='imagenet', include_top=False,
input_shape=(224, 224, 3))


# Freeze convolutional base
base_model.trainable = False


# Create new model on top of the pre-trained base
model = models.Sequential([
    base_model,
    layers.Flatten(),
    layers.Dense(256, activation='relu'),
    layers.Dropout(0.5),
    layers.Dense(1, activation='sigmoid')
])


# Compile the model
model.compile(optimizer=optimizers.RMSprop(lr=1e-4),
        loss='binary_crossentropy',
        metrics=['accuracy'])


# Data preprocessing
train_datagen = ImageDataGenerator(rescale=1./255, rotation_range=40,
                    width_shift_range=0.2, height_shift_range=0.2,
                    shear_range=0.2, zoom_range=0.2,
horizontal_flip=True,
                    fill_mode='nearest')
```

```python
test_datagen = ImageDataGenerator(rescale=1./255)


train_generator = train_datagen.flow_from_directory(
    train_dir,
    target_size=(224, 224),
    batch_size=20,
    class_mode='binary'
)

validation_generator = test_datagen.flow_from_directory(
    validation_dir,
    target_size=(224, 224),
    batch_size=20,
    class_mode='binary'
)

# Train the model
history = model.fit(
    train_generator,
    steps_per_epoch=100,
    epochs=30,
    validation_data=validation_generator,
    validation_steps=50
)
```

In this code:

- We first load the pre-trained VGG16 model without the top (fully connected) layers using **VGG16** from Keras applications.

- We freeze the convolutional base of the VGG16 model to prevent its weights from being updated during training on the new dataset.

- We construct a new model on top of the pre-trained base, adding new fully connected layers for fine-tuning on the new dataset.

- We compile the model with an appropriate optimizer and loss function.

- We perform data preprocessing using **ImageDataGenerator** to augment the training images and rescale pixel values.

- We train the model using the augmented data generated by the **train_generator** and validate it using the **validation_generator**.

This code demonstrates how to perform transfer learning by fine-tuning a pre-trained VGG16 model on a new dataset for a binary image classification task.

14.2 AutoML (Automated Machine Learning)

Introduction to AutoML:

AutoML, or Automated Machine Learning, encompasses a set of techniques and tools designed to automate the entire process of designing, training, and deploying machine learning models, thereby making machine learning more accessible to individuals with varying levels of expertise. It streamlines and accelerates the machine learning pipeline, covering aspects from data preprocessing and feature engineering to model selection, hyperparameter optimization, and model deployment. By automating repetitive and time-consuming tasks, AutoML democratizes the application of machine learning to real-world problems, enabling users with different levels of domain knowledge to utilize advanced analytical techniques more efficiently and effectively.

Key Components of AutoML:

- **Automated Model Selection:**

  - AutoML tools explore various algorithms and architectures to find the best-performing model for a given task.

- **Hyperparameter Tuning:**

  - Automatic optimization of hyperparameters to enhance model performance.

- **Feature Engineering:**

  - Automated creation and selection of features to improve model accuracy.

Components of AutoML:

1. **Data Preprocessing**: AutoML tools often include capabilities for automatically handling common data preprocessing tasks such as missing value imputation, feature scaling, encoding categorical variables, and handling outliers. This ensures that the input data is properly prepared for model training.

2. **Feature Engineering**: Feature engineering is a critical step in the machine learning pipeline, but it can be challenging and time-consuming. AutoML frameworks may incorporate automated feature engineering techniques such as feature selection, transformation, and generation to extract relevant information from the input data and improve model performance.

3. **Model Selection**: AutoML platforms typically provide a selection of machine learning algorithms and model architectures, allowing users to automatically choose the most suitable model for their dataset and task. These models may include traditional algorithms like decision trees and support vector machines, as well as deep learning architectures like convolutional neural networks and recurrent neural networks.

4. **Hyperparameter Optimization**: Hyperparameters significantly impact the performance of machine learning models, but tuning them manually can be tedious and inefficient. AutoML tools

leverage techniques such as grid search, random search, and Bayesian optimization to automatically search for the optimal hyperparameters that maximize the model's performance on a validation dataset.

5. **Ensemble Methods**: Ensemble methods, which combine multiple models to improve predictive performance, are commonly used in AutoML frameworks. These methods may include techniques such as bagging, boosting, and stacking, which combine predictions from multiple models to produce a more robust and accurate final prediction.

6. **Model Evaluation and Deployment**: AutoML platforms provide mechanisms for evaluating the performance of trained models on holdout datasets or through cross-validation. Once a satisfactory model is identified, AutoML tools often offer seamless deployment options, allowing users to deploy their models into production environments with minimal effort.

Benefits of AutoML:

- **Time and Resource Savings**: AutoML automates repetitive tasks and reduces the time and resources required to build and deploy machine learning models, enabling organizations to iterate more quickly and efficiently.

- **Accessibility**: AutoML democratizes machine learning by making it accessible to users with limited machine learning expertise. Users can leverage AutoML tools to build and deploy models without extensive knowledge of algorithms, programming, or data science principles.

- **Scalability**: AutoML frameworks are designed to scale with the complexity and size of the data, allowing organizations to apply machine learning techniques to large-scale datasets and complex problems.

- **Consistency and Reproducibility**: By automating the machine learning pipeline, AutoML ensures consistency and reproducibility across experiments, making it easier to track and compare model performance over time.

Considerations and Limitations:

- **Domain Expertise**: While AutoML simplifies many aspects of the machine learning process, domain expertise is still essential for interpreting results, selecting appropriate features, and ensuring that the model aligns with the requirements of the problem domain.

- **Black Box Models**: Some AutoML techniques may result in complex, black-box models that are difficult to interpret and explain. It's important to balance model performance with interpretability, especially in regulated industries or applications where model transparency is critical.

- **Customization and Flexibility**: AutoML frameworks may not always provide the flexibility and customization options required for specialized use cases or advanced machine learning techniques. Organizations may need to supplement AutoML with manual interventions or custom development to address specific requirements.

Popular AutoML Tools and Frameworks:

1. **Google Cloud AutoML**: A suite of machine learning products offered by Google Cloud Platform that enables users to train high-quality custom machine learning models with minimal effort and machine learning expertise.

2. **Auto-sklearn**: An automated machine learning toolkit based on scikit-learn that automatically searches for the best machine learning pipeline for a given dataset.

3. **H2O AutoML**: A platform from H2O.ai that automates the process of training and tuning machine learning models, including feature engineering, model selection, and hyperparameter optimization.

4. **TPOT (Tree-based Pipeline Optimization Tool)**: A Python library that automates the selection of machine learning pipelines using genetic programming, including preprocessing steps, feature selection, and model selection.

AutoML is a powerful approach to democratize machine learning, enabling organizations and individuals to leverage machine learning techniques without requiring extensive expertise or resources. By automating the machine learning pipeline, AutoML accelerates model development, improves model performance, and fosters innovation across industries.

Here's a basic example using Google Cloud AutoML Vision for image classification:

```python
from google.cloud import automl

# Authenticate to the AutoML API
client = automl.AutoMlClient.from_service_account_json('path/to/service_account.json')

# Set the project ID and model ID
project_id = 'your-project-id'
model_id = 'your-model-id'

# Get the prediction client
prediction_client = automl.PredictionServiceClient()

# Load an image for classification
image_path = 'path/to/image.jpg'
with open(image_path, 'rb') as image_file:
    content = image_file.read()

# Prepare the payload for prediction
payload = {"image": {"image_bytes": content}}
```

```python
# Make a prediction request

prediction_response =
prediction_client.predict(name=f'projects/{project_id}/locations/us-
central1/models/{model_id}', payload=payload)


# Print the top prediction

top_prediction = prediction_response.payload[0]

print(f'Predicted class: {top_prediction.display_name}')

print(f'Confidence: {top_prediction.classification.score}')
```

In this example:

- We first authenticate to the AutoML API using a service account JSON file.

- We specify the project ID and model ID corresponding to the trained AutoML Vision model.

- We load an image for classification and prepare the payload for prediction.

- We make a prediction request to the AutoML model using the **predict** method of the **PredictionServiceClient**.

- Finally, we print the top prediction class and its confidence score.

This code demonstrates how to use the Google Cloud AutoML API to perform image classification with a pre-trained model. You'll need to replace **'path/to/service_account.json'**, **'your-project-id'**, **'your-model-id'**, and **'path/to/image.jpg'** with the appropriate values for your project and environment.

14.3 Hyperparameter Tuning

Hyperparameter tuning is a crucial step in the machine learning pipeline that involves selecting the optimal set of hyperparameters for a given model and dataset. Hyperparameters are configuration settings that control the learning process and directly impact the performance of the model. Unlike model parameters, which are learned during training, hyperparameters are set before training begins and are typically chosen through experimentation and optimization.

Importance of Hyperparameter Tuning:

Hyperparameters play a significant role in determining the performance and generalization ability of machine learning models. Choosing appropriate values for hyperparameters can lead to models that converge faster, generalize better to unseen data, and achieve higher predictive accuracy. Conversely, suboptimal hyperparameters can result in models that underfit or overfit the training data, leading to poor performance on real-world tasks.

Common Hyperparameters:

1. **Learning Rate**: The learning rate determines the step size taken during gradient descent optimization. A higher learning rate may cause the optimization algorithm to overshoot the minimum, while a lower learning rate may result in slow convergence.

2. **Batch Size**: The batch size specifies the number of training examples used in each iteration of the optimization algorithm. Larger batch sizes can lead to faster convergence but may require more memory.

3. **Number of Layers**: For deep learning models, the number of layers and the size of each layer (number of neurons) are critical hyperparameters that influence the model's capacity to learn complex patterns from data.

4. **Activation Functions**: The choice of activation functions in neural networks, such as ReLU, sigmoid, or tanh, can significantly impact the model's ability to capture non-linear relationships in the data.

5. **Regularization Parameters**: Regularization techniques like L1 and L2 regularization introduce penalty terms to the loss function to prevent overfitting. The strength of regularization, controlled by hyperparameters like alpha (for L2 regularization) or lambda (for

L1 regularization), affects the trade-off between model complexity and generalization performance.

Hyperparameter Tuning Techniques:

1. **Grid Search**: Grid search involves defining a grid of hyperparameter values and evaluating the model's performance for each combination of hyperparameters. It systematically searches the entire hyperparameter space to identify the optimal configuration.

2. **Random Search**: Random search randomly samples hyperparameter values from predefined distributions and evaluates the model's performance. Compared to grid search, random search is more computationally efficient and often leads to better performance, especially in high-dimensional hyperparameter spaces.

3. **Bayesian Optimization**: Bayesian optimization is a probabilistic model-based approach that uses previous observations to guide the search for optimal hyperparameters. It builds a surrogate model of the objective function and uses it to intelligently select the next set of hyperparameters to evaluate.

4. **Gradient-based Optimization**: Some hyperparameters, such as the learning rate, can be optimized using gradient-based optimization techniques like stochastic gradient descent with adaptive learning rates (e.g., Adam, RMSprop). These techniques adjust the hyperparameters during training based on the gradients of the loss function with respect to the hyperparameters.

Best Practices for Hyperparameter Tuning:

1. **Start with Coarse Search**: Begin by exploring a wide range of hyperparameter values using coarse search techniques like random search. This helps identify promising regions of the hyperparameter space.

2. **Refine with Fine Search**: Once promising regions are identified, perform a more detailed search using techniques like grid search or Bayesian optimization to fine-tune the hyperparameters and maximize performance.

3. **Use Cross-Validation**: Evaluate the performance of different hyperparameter configurations using cross-validation to ensure robustness and avoid overfitting to the validation set.

4. **Monitor and Iterate**: Continuously monitor the performance of the model during hyperparameter tuning and iterate as needed to explore additional regions of the hyperparameter space.

Hyperparameter tuning is a critical aspect of the machine learning pipeline that can significantly impact the performance and effectiveness of machine learning models. By systematically searching the hyperparameter space and selecting optimal configurations, practitioners can build models that generalize well to unseen data and achieve state-of-the-art performance on real-world tasks.

Hyperparameters are configuration settings for machine learning models that are not learned from the data. Effective tuning of hyperparameters is crucial for optimizing model performance.

Techniques for Hyperparameter Tuning:

- **Grid Search:**
  - Exhaustively searches a predefined hyperparameter grid.

```
from sklearn.model_selection import GridSearchCV


param_grid = {'C': [0.1, 1, 10], 'kernel': ['linear', 'rbf']}
grid_search = GridSearchCV(SVC(), param_grid, cv=5)
grid_search.fit(X_train, y_train)
```

Random Search:
- Randomly samples hyperparameters from predefined distributions.

```
from sklearn.model_selection import RandomizedSearchCV
```

```
param_dist = {'C': [0.1, 1, 10], 'kernel': ['linear', 'rbf']}

random_search = RandomizedSearchCV(SVC(),
param_distributions=param_dist, n_iter=3, cv=5)

random_search.fit(X_train, y_train)
```

Bayesian Optimization:

- Utilizes probabilistic models to explore hyperparameter space efficiently.

```
from skopt import BayesSearchCV


opt_search = BayesSearchCV(SVC(), {'C': (0.1, 10.0, 'log-uniform'),
'kernel': ['linear', 'rbf']}, n_iter=32)

opt_search.fit(X_train, y_train)
```

Hyperparameter tuning is an ongoing process that involves experimenting with different configurations to find the optimal settings for a specific model and task. Automated approaches, such as Bayesian optimization or AutoML, can significantly simplify this process.

Here's an example of hyperparameter tuning using grid search with a support vector machine (SVM) classifier in Python using Scikit-learn:

```
from sklearn.datasets import load_iris

from sklearn.model_selection import train_test_split, GridSearchCV

from sklearn.svm import SVC


# Load the Iris dataset
```

```python
iris = load_iris()
X, y = iris.data, iris.target


# Split the dataset into training and testing sets
X_train, X_test, y_train, y_test = train_test_split(X, y, test_size=0.2,
random_state=42)


# Define the hyperparameters grid
param_grid = {
    'C': [0.1, 1, 10, 100],
    'gamma': [0.001, 0.01, 0.1, 1],
    'kernel': ['linear', 'rbf', 'poly']
}


# Create the SVM classifier
svm = SVC()


# Perform grid search with cross-validation
grid_search = GridSearchCV(estimator=svm, param_grid=param_grid,
cv=5, scoring='accuracy')
grid_search.fit(X_train, y_train)


# Print the best hyperparameters
print("Best hyperparameters:", grid_search.best_params_)


# Evaluate the best model on the test set
```

```
best_model = grid_search.best_estimator_
test_accuracy = best_model.score(X_test, y_test)
print("Test set accuracy:", test_accuracy)
```

In this example:

- We first load the Iris dataset and split it into training and testing sets.

- We define a grid of hyperparameters for the support vector machine (SVM) classifier, including the regularization parameter **C**, the kernel coefficient **gamma**, and the kernel type **kernel**.

- We create an SVM classifier and use **GridSearchCV** to perform grid search with 5-fold cross-validation to find the best hyperparameters.

- We print the best hyperparameters found by grid search.

- Finally, we evaluate the best model on the test set and print its accuracy.

This example demonstrates how to perform hyperparameter tuning using grid search with Scikit-learn. You can adjust the hyperparameters and the model to your specific use case and dataset.

Chapter 14 End-of-chapter Practice Problems

1. **Grid Search Practice:**

   - Use grid search to tune the hyperparameters of a decision tree classifier (**DecisionTreeClassifier**) for a classification task on a dataset of your choice. Experiment with different values for parameters like **max_depth**, **min_samples_split**, and **min_samples_leaf**. Evaluate the performance of the tuned model on a held-out test set.

2. **Random Search Practice:**

- Implement random search to tune the hyperparameters of a random forest classifier (**RandomForestClassifier**) for a classification task on the same dataset used in problem 1. Compare the results of random search with grid search in terms of computational efficiency and model performance.

3. **Bayesian Optimization Practice:**

   - Use a Bayesian optimization library such as **scikit-optimize** or **hyperopt** to tune the hyperparameters of a gradient boosting classifier (**GradientBoostingClassifier**) for a classification task. Experiment with different acquisition functions and optimization strategies. Evaluate the performance of the tuned model on a validation set.

4. **Advanced Practice:**

   - Explore more advanced hyperparameter tuning techniques such as population-based methods (e.g., genetic algorithms) or model-based optimization (e.g., Gaussian process-based methods). Implement one of these techniques to tune the hyperparameters of a machine learning model for a regression task on a dataset of your choice.

5. **Case Study:**

   - Apply hyperparameter tuning techniques to optimize the performance of a neural network model (e.g., multi-layer perceptron) for a classification or regression task. Experiment with different architectures, activation functions, learning rates, and regularization techniques. Compare the performance of the tuned model with the default settings.

These practice problems will help reinforce your understanding of hyperparameter tuning techniques and their practical applications in machine learning model optimization. Experiment with different datasets, algorithms, and hyperparameters to gain hands-on experience and improve your skills in hyperparameter optimization.

Chapter 15. Case Studies

In this section, we delve into real-world applications and case studies that illustrate the practical implementation of machine learning techniques across various domains. These case studies provide valuable insights into how machine learning algorithms can be utilized to solve complex problems and drive innovation in different industries.

1. Healthcare: Predictive Analytics for Disease Diagnosis

In the healthcare industry, machine learning plays a crucial role in predictive analytics for disease diagnosis. By analyzing medical data such as patient demographics, symptoms, and diagnostic tests, machine learning models can assist healthcare professionals in predicting the likelihood of diseases such as cancer, diabetes, and heart conditions. These predictive models aid in early detection, personalized treatment planning, and improving patient outcomes.

2. Finance: Fraud Detection in Financial Transactions

Financial institutions leverage machine learning algorithms for fraud detection in financial transactions. By analyzing patterns in transaction data, including transaction amounts, locations, and user behavior, machine learning models can identify fraudulent activities such as unauthorized access, identity theft, and payment fraud. These models help financial institutions mitigate risks, safeguard customer assets, and maintain trust in the financial system.

3. E-commerce: Recommender Systems for Personalized Recommendations

E-commerce platforms utilize recommender systems powered by machine learning to provide personalized product recommendations to users. By analyzing user browsing history, purchase behavior, and demographic information, these systems recommend relevant products that align with users' preferences and interests. This personalized approach enhances user experience, increases customer engagement, and drives sales revenue for e-commerce businesses.

4. Manufacturing: Predictive Maintenance for Equipment Failure Prediction

In the manufacturing sector, predictive maintenance using machine learning enables proactive identification of equipment failures before they occur. By analyzing sensor data, equipment performance metrics, and historical maintenance records, machine learning models can predict potential equipment failures, schedule preventive maintenance activities, and minimize downtime. This predictive maintenance approach improves operational efficiency, reduces maintenance costs, and extends the lifespan of manufacturing equipment.

5. Transportation: Autonomous Vehicles for Intelligent Transportation Systems

Autonomous vehicles powered by machine learning technologies are revolutionizing transportation systems worldwide. By leveraging sensors, cameras, and advanced algorithms, autonomous vehicles can perceive their surroundings, make real-time decisions, and navigate safely in complex traffic environments. These intelligent transportation systems promise to enhance road safety, reduce traffic congestion, and provide more efficient and sustainable mobility solutions for urban and rural communities.

6. Recommendation Systems: Personalizing Content

Online platforms, such as streaming services or e-commerce websites, use recommendation systems to provide personalized content to users. These systems leverage user preferences, historical interactions, and collaborative filtering techniques to recommend products, movies, or songs.

15.2 Walkthroughs of Complete Machine Learning Projects

Project: Image Classification with Convolutional Neural Networks (CNN)

Objective: Classify images into multiple categories using a CNN.

Steps:

1. **Data Preparation:**

   - Download and preprocess the dataset (e.g., CIFAR-10).

   - Split the data into training and testing sets.

2. **Model Building:**

- Define a CNN architecture using a deep learning framework (e.g., TensorFlow or PyTorch).
- Compile the model with an appropriate loss function and optimizer.

3. **Model Training:**
   - Train the model on the training dataset.
   - Monitor and adjust hyperparameters for optimal performance.

4. **Evaluation:**
   - Assess the model's performance on the testing dataset.
   - Analyze metrics such as accuracy, precision, and recall.

5. **Deployment:**
   - Save the trained model for future use.
   - Deploy the model in a web application or as part of a larger system.

Project: Predictive Maintenance for Equipment

Objective: Predict equipment failures in a manufacturing environment to enable proactive maintenance.

Steps:

1. **Data Collection:**
   - Gather historical sensor data from manufacturing equipment.
   - Include information on previous maintenance activities.

2. **Feature Engineering:**
   - Extract relevant features from the sensor data.
   - Create a target variable indicating the time to the next failure.

3. **Model Selection:**

   - Choose an appropriate machine learning model for time-to-event prediction (e.g., survival analysis).

4. **Hyperparameter Tuning:**

   - Optimize hyperparameters to improve model performance.

   - Utilize techniques like grid search or Bayesian optimization.

5. **Deployment:**

   - Integrate the predictive maintenance model into the manufacturing system.

Project: Predictive Analytics for Housing Prices:

Objective: Predict the prices of houses based on various features such as location, size, and amenities.

Steps:

1. **Data Collection:** Gather housing dataset from public sources or real estate agencies.

2. **Data Preprocessing:** Clean the data, handle missing values, and perform feature engineering.

3. **Exploratory Data Analysis (EDA):** Analyze the distribution of features, identify correlations, and visualize trends.

4. **Model Selection:** Choose appropriate regression algorithms (e.g., Linear Regression, Random Forest) for prediction.

5. **Model Training:** Train the selected models on the training dataset.

6. **Hyperparameter Tuning:** Optimize the hyperparameters of the models using techniques like grid search or random search.

7. **Model Evaluation:** Evaluate the performance of the models using metrics such as RMSE (Root Mean Squared Error) or MAE (Mean Absolute Error).

8. **Deployment:** Deploy the trained model into a web application or API for real-time predictions.

Project: Customer Churn Prediction in Telecom Industry:

Objective: Predict the likelihood of customers churning (leaving) a telecom service provider based on their usage patterns and demographics.

Steps:

1. **Data Collection:** Obtain customer data including usage statistics, subscription plans, and customer demographics.

2. **Data Preprocessing:** Clean the data, handle categorical variables, and encode features.

3. **Exploratory Data Analysis (EDA):** Analyze customer churn rates, identify influential factors, and visualize trends.

4. **Feature Engineering:** Extract relevant features and create new variables to improve model performance.

5. **Model Selection:** Choose classification algorithms (e.g., Logistic Regression, Gradient Boosting) for prediction.

6. **Model Training:** Train the selected models on the training dataset.

7. **Hyperparameter Tuning:** Optimize the hyperparameters of the models using techniques like grid search or Bayesian optimization.

8. **Model Evaluation:** Evaluate the performance of the models using metrics such as accuracy, precision, recall, and F1 score.

9. **Deployment:** Deploy the trained model into a production environment for monitoring and decision-making.

Project: Sentiment Analysis for Social Media Posts:

Objective: Analyze the sentiment (positive, negative, neutral) of social media posts or customer reviews.

Steps:

1. **Data Collection:** Gather social media posts or customer reviews from platforms like Twitter, Facebook, or Yelp.

2. **Data Preprocessing:** Clean the text data, remove stopwords, and perform tokenization.

3. **Feature Extraction:** Extract features from the text data using techniques like TF-IDF (Term Frequency-Inverse Document Frequency).

4. **Model Selection:** Choose classification algorithms (e.g., Naive Bayes, Support Vector Machines) for sentiment analysis.

5. **Model Training:** Train the selected models on the labeled dataset of social media posts.

6. **Model Evaluation:** Evaluate the performance of the models using metrics such as accuracy, precision, recall, and F1 score.

7. **Deployment:** Deploy the trained model into a web application or API for real-time sentiment analysis.

Below are sample code snippets for the provided examples:

Predictive Analytics for Housing Prices:

```
# Step 1: Data Collection
import pandas as pd
housing_data = pd.read_csv('housing_dataset.csv')


# Step 2: Data Preprocessing
# Clean the data, handle missing values, and perform feature engineering


# Step 3: Exploratory Data Analysis (EDA)
import seaborn as sns
import matplotlib.pyplot as plt
```

```python
sns.pairplot(housing_data, x_vars=['sqft', 'bedrooms', 'bathrooms'],
y_vars=['price'])

plt.show()


# Step 4: Model Selection
from sklearn.model_selection import train_test_split
from sklearn.linear_model import LinearRegression


X = housing_data[['sqft', 'bedrooms', 'bathrooms']]
y = housing_data['price']


X_train, X_test, y_train, y_test = train_test_split(X, y, test_size=0.2,
random_state=42)


model = LinearRegression()


# Step 5: Model Training
model.fit(X_train, y_train)


# Step 6: Hyperparameter Tuning
# No hyperparameters for Linear Regression, but can explore
regularization techniques for other algorithms


# Step 7: Model Evaluation
from sklearn.metrics import mean_squared_error
```

```python
y_pred = model.predict(X_test)

mse = mean_squared_error(y_test, y_pred)

print("Mean Squared Error:", mse)


# Step 8: Deployment

# Deploy the trained model into a web application or API for real-time
predictions
```

Customer Churn Prediction in Telecom Industry:

```python
# Step 1: Data Collection
import pandas as pd
customer_data = pd.read_csv('customer_churn_data.csv')


# Step 2: Data Preprocessing
# Clean the data, handle missing values, and encode categorical variables


# Step 3: Exploratory Data Analysis (EDA)
import seaborn as sns
import matplotlib.pyplot as plt


sns.countplot(x='Churn', data=customer_data)
plt.show()


# Step 4: Feature Engineering
# Extract relevant features and create new variables


# Step 5: Model Selection
from sklearn.model_selection import train_test_split
from sklearn.ensemble import RandomForestClassifier


X = customer_data.drop(columns=['Churn'])
y = customer_data['Churn']
```

```python
X_train, X_test, y_train, y_test = train_test_split(X, y, test_size=0.2, random_state=42)


model = RandomForestClassifier()

# Step 6: Model Training
model.fit(X_train, y_train)

# Step 7: Hyperparameter Tuning
# Optimize hyperparameters using techniques like grid search or random search

# Step 8: Model Evaluation
from sklearn.metrics import accuracy_score, classification_report

y_pred = model.predict(X_test)
accuracy = accuracy_score(y_test, y_pred)
print("Accuracy:", accuracy)
print(classification_report(y_test, y_pred))

# Step 9: Deployment
# Deploy the trained model into a production environment for monitoring and decision-making
```

Sentiment Analysis for Social Media Posts:

```python
# Step 1: Data Collection
```

```python
import pandas as pd
social_media_data = pd.read_csv('social_media_posts.csv')


# Step 2: Data Preprocessing
# Clean the text data, remove stopwords, and perform tokenization


# Step 3: Feature Extraction
from sklearn.feature_extraction.text import TfidfVectorizer


tfidf_vectorizer = TfidfVectorizer()
X = tfidf_vectorizer.fit_transform(social_media_data['text'])
y = social_media_data['sentiment']


# Step 4: Model Selection
from sklearn.model_selection import train_test_split
from sklearn.naive_bayes import MultinomialNB


X_train, X_test, y_train, y_test = train_test_split(X, y, test_size=0.2,
random_state=42)


model = MultinomialNB()

# Step 5: Model Training
model.fit(X_train, y_train)
```

```
# Step 6: Model Evaluation

from sklearn.metrics import accuracy_score, classification_report


y_pred = model.predict(X_test)

accuracy = accuracy_score(y_test, y_pred)

print("Accuracy:", accuracy)

print(classification_report(y_test, y_pred))


# Step 7: Deployment

# Deploy the trained model into a web application or API for real-time
sentiment analysis
```

These code snippets illustrate the implementation of machine learning
models for the provided examples. Each snippet covers data preprocessing,
model training, evaluation, and deployment steps as outlined in the
respective project walkthroughs.

Chapter 15 end-of-chapter problems

Predictive Analytics for Housing Prices:

1. **Feature Engineering:** Explore additional features such as
   proximity to amenities or neighborhood crime rates. How do these
   new features affect the model's performance?

2. **Model Comparison:** Compare the performance of Linear
   Regression with other regression algorithms such as Decision
   Trees or Random Forests. Which algorithm yields the best results?

3. **Advanced Visualization:** Visualize the model's predictions on a
   map using geographical coordinates. How does the spatial
   distribution of predicted prices compare to actual prices?

Customer Churn Prediction in Telecom Industry:

4. **Feature Importance:** Identify the most important features contributing to customer churn prediction using the trained Random Forest model. How do these features align with domain knowledge?

5. **Imbalanced Data Handling:** The dataset may have imbalanced classes (churners vs. non-churners). Implement techniques like oversampling or undersampling to address this issue and reevaluate model performance.

6. **Cost-Benefit Analysis:** Conduct a cost-benefit analysis to determine the potential financial impact of reducing churn based on model predictions.

Sentiment Analysis for Social Media Posts:

7. **Model Fine-Tuning:** Experiment with different text preprocessing techniques such as stemming or lemmatization. How do these techniques affect the model's accuracy?

8. **Multi-Class Classification:** Extend the sentiment analysis task to handle more than three sentiment classes (e.g., positive, negative, neutral, and mixed). Evaluate the model's performance on the expanded dataset.

9. **Transfer Learning:** Explore the use of pre-trained word embeddings (e.g., Word2Vec or GloVe) to improve the model's performance on sentiment analysis.

Chapter 16. Ethical Considerations

As the field of machine learning continues to advance, it is imperative to address the ethical implications associated with its development, deployment, and impact on society. Ethical considerations in machine learning encompass various aspects, including bias and fairness, as well as the adoption of responsible AI practices. In this section, we explore these crucial dimensions, shedding light on the ethical responsibilities that come with harnessing the power of machine learning.

16.1 Bias and Fairness in Machine Learning

Ethical considerations are crucial in machine learning to ensure fairness, transparency, and accountability in algorithmic decision-making processes. While machine learning models have the potential to generate valuable insights and improve efficiency in various domains, they can also perpetuate or exacerbate societal biases if not carefully designed and implemented. Two key aspects of ethical considerations in machine learning are bias and fairness.

Bias in Machine Learning:

Bias in machine learning refers to systematic errors or inaccuracies in algorithms that result in unfair treatment of certain individuals or groups. Bias can manifest in various forms, including:

- **Algorithmic Bias:** Bias inherent in the design or structure of machine learning algorithms, leading to unequal treatment based on sensitive attributes such as race, gender, or socioeconomic status.

- **Data Bias:** Bias introduced by skewed or incomplete training data, resulting in models that reflect historical inequalities or stereotypes present in the data.

- **User Bias:** Bias introduced through user interactions or feedback, leading to feedback loops that reinforce existing biases in recommendation systems or personalized services.

Identifying and mitigating bias in machine learning requires careful examination of data collection, model development, and deployment processes. Strategies for addressing bias include:

- **Diverse and Representative Data Collection:** Ensure that training data adequately represents the diversity of the population and includes sufficient samples from underrepresented groups.

- **Fairness-aware Algorithms:** Develop algorithms that explicitly incorporate fairness constraints or metrics to mitigate bias and ensure equitable outcomes across different demographic groups.

- **Bias Detection and Mitigation Techniques:** Employ techniques such as fairness-aware learning, adversarial debiasing, or bias audits to detect and mitigate bias in models.

Fairness in Machine Learning:

Fairness in machine learning refers to the equitable treatment of individuals or groups, ensuring that algorithmic decisions do not discriminate or disadvantage particular demographics. Fairness considerations often involve defining and operationalizing fairness metrics tailored to specific use cases or applications. Common fairness notions include:

- **Individual Fairness:** Ensuring that similar individuals receive similar predictions or treatment from the model, regardless of their sensitive attributes.

- **Group Fairness:** Ensuring that predictions or outcomes are equitable across predefined demographic groups, such as race, gender, or age.

- **Intersectional Fairness:** Considering the intersection of multiple protected attributes to address unique challenges faced by individuals belonging to multiple marginalized groups.

Achieving fairness in machine learning requires a holistic approach that considers not only technical aspects but also ethical, legal, and social implications. Transparency, accountability, and stakeholder engagement are essential for promoting fairness and building trust in machine learning systems.

16.2 Responsible AI Practices

Responsible AI practices encompass a set of principles and guidelines aimed at ensuring the ethical and responsible development, deployment, and use of artificial intelligence (AI) systems. As AI technologies continue to evolve and integrate into various aspects of society, it is essential to prioritize ethical considerations and adopt practices that prioritize the well-being of individuals and communities.

Core Principles of Responsible AI:

1. **Transparency:** AI systems should be transparent, with clear documentation and explanations of their functionality, decision-making processes, and potential impacts. Transparency enables users to understand how AI systems work and assess their reliability and fairness.

2. **Accountability:** Stakeholders involved in the development and deployment of AI systems should be accountable for their decisions and actions. Accountability entails taking responsibility for the outcomes of AI systems, addressing any unintended consequences, and ensuring compliance with legal and ethical standards.

3. **Fairness and Equity:** AI systems should be designed and deployed in a manner that promotes fairness and equity, avoiding bias and discrimination against individuals or groups based on characteristics such as race, gender, or socioeconomic status. Fairness considerations should be integrated into all stages of the AI lifecycle, from data collection and model training to deployment and monitoring.

4. **Privacy and Data Protection:** Respect for privacy and data protection rights is paramount in AI development. AI systems should adhere to relevant privacy regulations and standards, safeguarding the confidentiality, integrity, and accessibility of personal data. Data minimization, anonymization, and informed consent are essential principles for responsible data handling.

5. **Safety and Reliability:** AI systems should prioritize safety and reliability to minimize the risk of harm to users and society. Robust testing, validation, and risk assessment procedures should be implemented to identify and mitigate potential safety hazards or

failures. Human oversight and intervention mechanisms should be available to address unforeseen situations or errors.

6. **Human-Centered Design:** AI systems should be designed with a focus on human well-being and user needs. Human-centered design principles, such as inclusivity, accessibility, and usability, should guide the development process to ensure that AI technologies enhance human capabilities and empower individuals.

Implementation of Responsible AI Practices:

1. **Ethical AI Governance:** Establish clear policies, guidelines, and governance structures for overseeing the ethical development and deployment of AI systems within organizations. Ethical review boards, cross-functional teams, and external advisory groups can provide oversight and guidance on ethical issues.

2. **Ethical Risk Assessment:** Conduct comprehensive ethical risk assessments to identify potential ethical risks, biases, and unintended consequences associated with AI systems. Evaluate the social, cultural, and environmental impacts of AI applications and develop mitigation strategies to address identified risks.

3. **Continuous Monitoring and Evaluation:** Implement mechanisms for ongoing monitoring, evaluation, and auditing of AI systems to assess their performance, fairness, and compliance with ethical standards. Regular reviews and feedback loops enable organizations to identify and address ethical issues as they arise and evolve over time.

4. **Stakeholder Engagement:** Foster open dialogue and collaboration with stakeholders, including users, communities, policymakers, and advocacy groups, to solicit feedback, address concerns, and incorporate diverse perspectives into AI decision-making processes. Engaging stakeholders throughout the AI lifecycle promotes transparency, accountability, and trust.

5. **Education and Awareness:** Promote education and awareness initiatives to increase understanding of responsible AI practices among developers, policymakers, and the general public. Training programs, workshops, and resources on ethical AI design,

implementation, and governance empower stakeholders to make informed decisions and uphold ethical standards.

Adopting responsible AI practices is essential for harnessing the transformative potential of AI while minimizing risks and ensuring equitable and ethical outcomes for society. By prioritizing transparency, accountability, fairness, and human-centered design, organizations can build trust, foster innovation, and promote the responsible use of AI technologies for the benefit of all.

Chapter 17. Future Trends

The landscape of machine learning is dynamic, constantly evolving with advancements in technology, research, and societal needs. In this section, we explore the emerging trends in machine learning and the ongoing developments in ethical and responsible AI practices that are shaping the future of this field.

17.1 Emerging Trends in Machine Learning

17.1.1. Federated Learning

Federated learning is a decentralized approach to training machine learning models across multiple devices or servers while keeping data localized and secure. In federated learning, model updates are computed locally on user devices or edge devices, and only aggregated model parameters are shared with a central server. This paradigm enables collaborative model training without centralizing sensitive data, making it particularly suitable for privacy-sensitive applications such as healthcare, finance, and IoT devices.

Models are trained across decentralized devices or servers without exchanging raw data, allowing for collaborative learning while protecting sensitive information.

17.1.2. Explainable AI (XAI)

As machine learning models become more complex, the demand for transparency in decision-making is growing. Explainable AI aims to provide insights into how models arrive at specific predictions, enhancing trust and facilitating the interpretation of model outcomes.

Explainable AI, or XAI, is an emerging trend focused on developing machine learning models that can provide interpretable explanations for their predictions and decisions. XAI techniques aim to enhance transparency, accountability, and trust in AI systems by enabling users to understand and reason about model behavior. Methods such as attention mechanisms, feature importance analysis, and model-agnostic explanations are being actively researched and applied to improve the interpretability of complex machine learning models.

17.1.3. Reinforcement Learning Advancements

Reinforcement Learning continues to be a focus of research, with ongoing developments in areas such as deep reinforcement learning, meta-learning, and more robust algorithms. These advancements are opening new possibilities for applications in robotics, gaming, and autonomous systems.

17.1.4. Edge Computing Integration

The integration of machine learning with edge computing devices is becoming more prevalent. This trend enables real-time processing and decision-making on devices, reducing latency and dependency on centralized cloud infrastructures.

17.1.5. Quantum Machine Learning

The intersection of quantum computing and machine learning holds promise for solving complex problems that classical computers struggle with. Quantum machine learning algorithms are being explored for tasks like optimization, simulation, and pattern recognition.

17.1.6. Meta-Learning

Meta-learning, also known as learning to learn, is a subfield of machine learning focused on developing algorithms that can learn new tasks or domains quickly and efficiently. Meta-learning techniques aim to generalize across tasks by leveraging prior knowledge or experience from related tasks. By enabling models to adapt and generalize more effectively to new situations, meta-learning has the potential to accelerate learning and improve the robustness of machine learning systems.

17.1.7. Ethical AI and Responsible AI Governance

Ethical AI and responsible AI governance are becoming increasingly important as society grapples with the ethical, social, and legal implications of AI technologies. Future trends in this area include the development of ethical AI frameworks, regulations, and standards to ensure that AI systems are designed, deployed, and used in a manner that aligns with societal values and promotes human well-being. Responsible AI governance mechanisms, such as AI impact assessments, algorithmic auditing, and transparency requirements, are also likely to play a critical role in mitigating risks and promoting trust in AI systems.

17.1.8. Continual Learning

Continual learning, or lifelong learning, is a research area focused on developing machine learning models that can continuously acquire new knowledge and adapt to changing environments over time. Continual learning techniques enable models to learn from streaming data, adapt to concept drift, and retain knowledge from past experiences without catastrophic forgetting. As AI applications become more dynamic and interactive, continual learning approaches are expected to become increasingly important for building adaptive and resilient AI systems.

17.2 Ethical AI and Responsible AI Developments

17.2.1. Regulatory Frameworks

The development and implementation of regulatory frameworks for AI are gaining momentum. Governments and organizations worldwide are working to establish guidelines that govern the ethical use of AI, addressing issues such as bias, transparency, and accountability.

17.2.2. Bias Detection and Mitigation Tools

With increased awareness of the impact of bias in AI systems, there is a growing emphasis on developing tools and techniques for detecting and mitigating bias. Automated bias detection algorithms and ethical guidelines are becoming integral parts of the AI development lifecycle.

17.2.3. Continued Emphasis on Responsible AI Education

Educational initiatives focused on responsible AI practices are on the rise. As the ethical implications of AI become more apparent, there is a growing need for training programs, certifications, and resources to educate developers, data scientists, and decision-makers on responsible AI principles.

17.2.4. AI for Social Good

The use of AI for social good is gaining prominence, with initiatives addressing global challenges such as climate change, healthcare accessibility, and disaster response. Ethical considerations are at the forefront of these initiatives to ensure positive societal impact.

17.2.5. Human-AI Collaboration

The future envisions closer collaboration between humans and AI systems. Designing AI technologies that complement human skills, enhance productivity, and respect human autonomy is a key focus area for ethical and responsible AI development.

17.2.6. Ethical AI Principles

Ethical AI principles serve as guiding frameworks for the development, deployment, and use of AI technologies. These principles, which may vary across organizations and contexts, typically include values such as fairness, transparency, accountability, privacy, and human dignity. By adhering to ethical AI principles, developers and practitioners can ensure that AI systems are designed and implemented in a manner that prioritizes the well-being and rights of individuals and communities.

17.2.7. Responsible AI Governance

Responsible AI governance involves establishing policies, guidelines, and mechanisms for overseeing the ethical development, deployment, and use of AI systems within organizations and society at large. This includes defining roles and responsibilities, implementing ethical review processes, conducting risk assessments, and ensuring compliance with relevant regulations and standards. Responsible AI governance mechanisms help to foster transparency, accountability, and trust in AI technologies while mitigating potential ethical and societal risks.

17.2.8. Ethical AI Frameworks

Ethical AI frameworks provide structured approaches for addressing ethical considerations and dilemmas in AI development and deployment. These frameworks typically include principles, guidelines, and best practices for identifying and mitigating potential biases, discrimination, and unintended consequences in AI systems. Examples of ethical AI frameworks include the IEEE Ethically Aligned Design, the EU's Ethics Guidelines for Trustworthy AI, and industry-specific guidelines developed by organizations such as the Partnership on AI and the AI Ethics Lab.

17.2.9. Technological Solutions for Ethical AI

Technological solutions are being developed to support ethical AI practices and mitigate potential risks associated with AI systems. These solutions include techniques for bias detection and mitigation, fairness-aware machine learning algorithms, interpretability and explainability tools, privacy-preserving AI techniques, and adversarial robustness methods. By integrating these technological solutions into AI development pipelines, organizations can enhance the ethical robustness and accountability of their AI systems.

17.2.10. Community Engagement and Collaboration

Community engagement and collaboration are essential for promoting ethical AI and responsible AI development. This involves fostering dialogue and collaboration among diverse stakeholders, including researchers, practitioners, policymakers, ethicists, advocacy groups, and affected communities. By soliciting input, addressing concerns, and incorporating diverse perspectives into AI decision-making processes, organizations can build trust, promote inclusivity, and ensure that AI technologies serve the broader interests of society.

Conclusion:

Ethical AI and responsible AI developments are critical for ensuring that AI technologies are deployed and used in a manner that promotes human well-being, equity, and justice. By embracing ethical principles, implementing responsible governance mechanisms, leveraging technological solutions, and fostering collaboration, we can harness the transformative potential of AI while minimizing risks and maximizing benefits for individuals and communities.

As machine learning continues to evolve, several emerging trends are shaping the future of the field. These trends represent areas of innovation and research that are likely to have a significant impact on the development and application of machine learning techniques in various domains.

Chapter 18. Hands-On Projects

In this section, we provide a series of practical projects and exercises designed to empower readers to apply their knowledge of Python machine learning concepts. These hands-on activities are crafted to reinforce key concepts, enhance coding skills, and build a strong foundation in implementing machine learning solutions.

18.1 Project 1: Predictive Analytics with Regression

Objective: Build a predictive model using regression algorithms to analyze and predict trends in a real-world dataset. This project will involve data preprocessing, model training, and evaluation.

Steps:

1. **Dataset Selection:** Choose a dataset suitable for regression analysis, such as housing prices, stock prices, or any numeric prediction task.

2. **Data Exploration:** Perform exploratory data analysis (EDA) to understand the distribution of features and relationships within the dataset.

3. **Data Preprocessing:** Clean the data by handling missing values, scaling features, and encoding categorical variables.

4. **Model Selection:** Choose and implement regression algorithms (e.g., Linear Regression, Decision Tree Regression) using a machine learning library like Scikit-learn.

5. **Model Training:** Train the selected models on the training data and evaluate their performance.

6. **Hyperparameter Tuning:** Experiment with hyperparameter tuning to optimize the model's performance.

7. **Results Interpretation:** Interpret the results, analyze the model's predictions, and visualize the regression line.

18.2 Project 2: Image Classification with Convolutional Neural Networks (CNN)

Objective: Implement an image classification project using a Convolutional Neural Network (CNN). This project involves working with image data, building a CNN architecture, and training the model for accurate image recognition.

Steps:

1. **Dataset Selection:** Choose an image dataset with labeled classes, such as the CIFAR-10 dataset or a custom dataset relevant to your domain.

2. **Data Augmentation:** Apply data augmentation techniques to increase the diversity of the training dataset.

3. **Model Architecture:** Design a CNN architecture using a deep learning framework like TensorFlow or PyTorch.

4. **Model Training:** Train the CNN model on the labeled dataset, monitoring its performance on both training and validation sets.

5. **Model Evaluation:** Evaluate the model on a test set to assess its accuracy, precision, recall, and other relevant metrics.

6. **Fine-Tuning:** Experiment with hyperparameter tuning and model fine-tuning to enhance performance.

7. **Visualization:** Visualize the learned features and activations of the CNN to gain insights into its decision-making process.

18.3 Exercise Set: Reinforcement Learning

Objective: Gain hands-on experience with reinforcement learning by working on a set of exercises that involve training agents to perform tasks in various environments.

Exercises:

1. **CartPole Environment:** Implement a basic reinforcement learning agent to balance a pole on a moving cart using the OpenAI Gym's CartPole environment.

2. **Mountain Car Problem:** Solve the Mountain Car problem, where an agent must learn to drive a car up a steep hill using reinforcement learning techniques.

3. **Lunar Lander Game:** Develop a reinforcement learning agent capable of landing a lunar module safely on the moon's surface in the Lunar Lander environment.

4. **Deep Q-Network (DQN):** Implement a Deep Q-Network for more complex tasks, such as playing Atari games, demonstrating the power of deep reinforcement learning.

These hands-on projects and exercises are designed to reinforce theoretical concepts and provide practical experience in applying machine learning techniques. Readers are encouraged to experiment, modify parameters, and explore additional datasets to deepen their understanding of Python machine learning.

Chapter 19: Advanced Data Visualization Techniques

Advanced data visualization techniques go beyond basic plotting to offer deeper insights into complex datasets. These techniques leverage sophisticated methods to enhance the clarity, interactivity, and effectiveness of visual representations, helping analysts and decision-makers extract actionable insights from data.

1. Advanced Plotting with Matplotlib

Conceptual Overview: Matplotlib is a powerful library in Python for creating static, interactive, and animated visualizations. Advanced plotting techniques with Matplotlib involve customizing plots to present data in more meaningful ways and adding layers of complexity to visualize intricate patterns.

Key Concepts:

- **Subplots and Grids:** Utilize subplots to display multiple plots in a single figure, facilitating comparative analysis of different data dimensions or subsets. Grids can help in organizing complex visualizations.

- **Customizations:** Tailor visualizations by modifying colors, markers, line styles, and annotations. This customization enhances the readability and aesthetic appeal of the plots.

- **3D Plotting:** Create three-dimensional plots to represent data with three variables, providing additional insights into complex relationships.

Applications:

- Comparative analysis of multiple datasets.

- Detailed exploration of multidimensional data.

2. Interactive Visualizations with Plotly

Conceptual Overview: Plotly is a versatile library for creating interactive plots that allow users to engage with the data dynamically. Interactive visualizations enable users to explore data through zooming, panning, and filtering, which can reveal patterns not immediately apparent in static plots.

Key Concepts:

- **Interactive Features:** Incorporate features like tooltips, hover effects, and clickable elements that provide additional information or drill down into specific data points.

- **Dashboards:** Build interactive dashboards that combine multiple plots and controls, enabling users to explore different aspects of the data through a unified interface.

- **Real-Time Updates:** Utilize Plotly's capabilities to create visualizations that update in real-time, reflecting changes in the underlying data dynamically.

Applications:

- Exploratory data analysis.

- User-driven insights and data interaction.

3. Geospatial Data Visualization

Conceptual Overview: Geospatial data visualization involves representing data with geographic or spatial components on maps. This technique is essential for understanding spatial patterns, distributions, and relationships in data.

Key Concepts:

- **Maps and Overlays:** Use maps to plot data points, regions, or paths. Overlays can highlight specific areas or add layers of information, such as demographic data or infrastructure.

- **Choropleth Maps:** Display data through color gradients on geographic regions to show variations in metrics like population density or economic activity.

- **Geospatial Analysis:** Incorporate spatial analysis techniques to assess patterns like clustering, proximity, or spatial correlations.

Applications:

- Geographic distribution analysis.

- Spatial trend identification and regional insights.

4. Network Visualization

Conceptual Overview: Network visualization involves representing relationships and connections between entities in a network. This technique is useful for analyzing complex networks such as social networks, communication networks, or biological networks.

Key Concepts:

- **Node and Edge Representation:** Visualize entities (nodes) and their relationships (edges) to understand network structure and dynamics.

- **Graph Metrics:** Use metrics such as centrality, connectivity, and clustering coefficients to analyze network properties and identify key nodes or substructures.

- **Interactive Exploration:** Implement interactive features to explore different parts of the network, zoom in on clusters, or highlight specific connections.

Applications:

- Social network analysis.

- Communication flow and influence patterns

Advanced data visualization techniques encompass a range of methods that enhance the ability to interpret and analyze complex data. These include advanced plotting with Matplotlib for detailed and customizable visualizations, interactive features with Plotly for dynamic data exploration, geospatial data visualization for spatial insights, and network visualization for understanding relationships within complex networks. By leveraging these techniques, analysts can gain deeper insights and communicate findings more effectively.

Advanced Plotting with Matplotlib

Matplotlib is a versatile and powerful library for creating static, animated, and interactive visualizations in Python. This section will explore advanced plotting techniques using Matplotlib to help you create more sophisticated and informative visualizations.

1. Customizing Plot Styles

Matplotlib allows extensive customization of plots. You can modify colors, line styles, markers, and more. The style module provides predefined styles that can be easily applied to your plots.

Example: Customizing Plot Styles

```python
import matplotlib.pyplot as plt

# Use a predefined style
plt.style.use('seaborn-darkgrid')

x = range(10)
y = [i**2 for i in x]

plt.plot(x, y, color='purple', linestyle='--', marker='o', markersize=10)
plt.title('Customized Plot Styles')
plt.xlabel('X-axis')
plt.ylabel('Y-axis')
plt.grid(True)
plt.show()
```

2. Advanced Plot Types

Matplotlib supports a wide variety of plot types, including:

- **Subplots**: Combine multiple plots in a single figure using subplot or subplots.

Example: Creating Subplots

```
fig, axs = plt.subplots(2, 2, figsize=(10, 8))


# First subplot
axs[0, 0].plot(x, y, 'r--')
axs[0, 0].set_title('Red Dashed Line')


# Second subplot
axs[0, 1].bar(x, y, color='blue')
axs[0, 1].set_title('Bar Plot')


# Third subplot
axs[1, 0].scatter(x, y, color='green')
axs[1, 0].set_title('Scatter Plot')


# Fourth subplot
axs[1, 1].hist(y, bins=5, color='orange')
axs[1, 1].set_title('Histogram')


for ax in axs.flat:
    ax.label_outer()
```

```
plt.tight_layout()
plt.show()
```

- **Heatmaps**: Display data in matrix form with color-coding.

Example: Creating a Heatmap
```
import numpy as np
import seaborn as sns

data = np.random.rand(10, 12)
sns.heatmap(data, cmap='viridis', annot=True)
plt.title('Heatmap Example')
plt.show()
```

3. Adding Annotations and Text

Annotations and text help to provide context and emphasize important points in your plots.

Example: Adding Annotations
```
plt.plot(x, y, 'b-o')
plt.title('Plot with Annotations')
plt.xlabel('X-axis')
plt.ylabel('Y-axis')

# Adding annotation
plt.annotate('Peak', xy=(x[5], y[5]), xytext=(x[5]+1, y[5]*0.8),
             arrowprops=dict(facecolor='black', shrink=0.05),
```

```
            fontsize=12, color='red')


plt.grid(True)

plt.show()
```

4. Creating Interactive Plots

While Matplotlib is primarily used for static plots, it can be integrated with interactive plotting libraries like mplcursors for adding interactivity.

Example: Adding Interactivity with mplcursors

```
import mplcursors


fig, ax = plt.subplots()

scatter = ax.scatter(x, y)


mplcursors.cursor(scatter, hover=True)


plt.title('Interactive Scatter Plot')

plt.xlabel('X-axis')

plt.ylabel('Y-axis')

plt.show()
```

5. Saving and Exporting Plots

You can save your plots in various formats (e.g., PNG, PDF) using savefig.

Example: Saving a Plot

```
plt.plot(x, y, 'b-o')

plt.title('Plot to Save')
```

```
plt.xlabel('X-axis')

plt.ylabel('Y-axis')

plt.grid(True)


# Save the plot

plt.savefig('plot_example.png', dpi=300)

plt.show()
```

These advanced plotting techniques will help you create more detailed and customized visualizations using Matplotlib. By leveraging these tools, you can make your data presentations more effective and engaging.

Interactive Visualizations with Plotly

Interactive visualizations are essential for exploring data dynamically, allowing users to engage with visual elements in real-time. Plotly is a powerful Python library that excels in creating interactive plots with rich features. This section explores key concepts and techniques for utilizing Plotly to develop engaging visualizations.

1. Introduction to Plotly

Plotly is an open-source graphing library that enables the creation of interactive, publication-quality graphs. Unlike static visualizations, Plotly plots support user interactions such as zooming, panning, and hover effects. This interactivity enhances data exploration and presentation, making it easier to gain insights from complex datasets.

2. Creating Interactive Plots

Plotly provides a variety of plot types that support interactivity. Some common types include:

- **Line Charts**: Line charts in Plotly can be customized with interactive features such as hover information, tooltips, and clickable points. These features help users understand trends and data points more effectively.

- **Scatter Plots**: Scatter plots in Plotly allow users to interactively explore the relationship between two continuous variables. You can add interactive elements like hover labels and click events to provide additional data insights.

- **Bar Charts**: Bar charts created with Plotly can display additional information on hover, enabling users to see exact values and categories interactively. This is useful for comparing discrete data points.

3. Adding Interactivity

Plotly allows you to enhance plots with various interactive features:

- **Hover Effects**: Hover effects display additional information when users hover over data points. You can customize hover labels to show detailed data or context-specific information.

- **Zoom and Pan**: Plotly plots support zooming and panning, allowing users to focus on specific areas of the plot. This feature is particularly useful for large datasets or detailed visualizations.

- **Dropdown Menus**: Dropdown menus can be added to plots to allow users to select different data views or parameters. This interactivity enables users to filter or switch between different aspects of the data dynamically.

- **Buttons and Sliders**: Buttons and sliders can be integrated into Plotly plots to control aspects of the visualization, such as changing data ranges or updating plot types. This enhances user engagement and exploration.

4. Plotly Express vs. Plotly Graph Objects

Plotly offers two main ways to create interactive visualizations:

- **Plotly Express**: A high-level interface for creating plots with less code. It is ideal for quickly generating interactive plots with straightforward customization.

- **Plotly Graph Objects**: A more flexible and detailed interface for creating and customizing plots. It allows for extensive control over plot elements and interactivity, making it suitable for complex visualizations.

5. Exporting and Sharing Interactive Plots

Plotly plots can be saved and shared in various formats. Interactive plots can be exported as HTML files that maintain their interactive features when viewed in a web browser. Additionally, Plotly provides options for integrating plots into web applications or dashboards using frameworks like Dash.

Example Code

Here's a basic example demonstrating how to create an interactive scatter plot with Plotly Express:

```python
import plotly.express as px
import pandas as pd

# Sample data
data = pd.DataFrame({
    'x': [1, 2, 3, 4, 5],
    'y': [10, 15, 13, 17, 19],
    'label': ['A', 'B', 'C', 'D', 'E']
})

# Create interactive scatter plot
fig = px.scatter(data, x='x', y='y', text='label',
            title='Interactive Scatter Plot',
            labels={'x': 'X Axis', 'y': 'Y Axis'})
```

```python
# Update layout for hover effect
fig.update_traces(marker=dict(size=12, color='LightSkyBlue',
opacity=0.8),

            selector=dict(mode='markers+text'))


# Show the plot
fig.show()
```

This example demonstrates how to create a scatter plot with interactive hover effects using Plotly Express. By customizing the plot, you can enhance user experience and provide meaningful insights through interactivity.

Interactive visualizations with Plotly offer powerful ways to engage users and present data effectively. Mastering these techniques will enable you to create dynamic, user-friendly visualizations that enhance data exploration and communication.

Geospatial Data Visualization

1. Overview of Geospatial Data Visualization

Geospatial data visualization involves representing data related to geographic locations on maps or other spatial formats. This type of visualization is crucial for understanding spatial patterns, relationships, and trends within datasets that have a geographical component. Geospatial visualizations help in analyzing phenomena such as population distribution, climate patterns, traffic flows, and more.

2. Importance of Geospatial Visualization

Geospatial data visualization enables users to:

- **Identify Spatial Patterns**: Visualizing data on maps helps to identify geographical patterns and clusters, such as areas with high crime rates or regions with high sales volumes.

- **Understand Relationships**: It provides insights into the relationships between different geographic entities, such as proximity to facilities or regional demographics.

- **Make Informed Decisions**: Geographic visualizations support decision-making in various fields, including urban planning, disaster management, and resource allocation.

3. Tools and Libraries for Geospatial Visualization

Several tools and libraries are available for creating geospatial visualizations:

- **Geopandas**: An extension of the Pandas library that allows for easy manipulation and analysis of geospatial data. It integrates well with libraries such as Matplotlib and Folium for visualization.

- **Folium**: A Python library used for creating interactive maps. It is built on the Leaflet.js JavaScript library and is useful for embedding maps with markers, popups, and choropleths.

- **Plotly**: Supports interactive geospatial plots through its plotly.express module. It provides functionalities for creating choropleth maps, scatter plots on maps, and more.

- **Mapbox**: A powerful tool for creating custom and interactive maps. It offers a rich set of APIs and libraries for building sophisticated geospatial visualizations.

4. Types of Geospatial Visualizations

- **Choropleth Maps**: Display data by shading geographic regions according to data values. They are useful for visualizing regional statistics, such as population density or election results.

- **Heat Maps**: Represent data density or intensity with color gradients. They are effective for showing concentrations of events or activities, such as traffic accidents or user activity hotspots.

- **Scatter Plots on Maps**: Plot individual data points on a map, allowing for the visualization of distributions and patterns. They are often used to display locations of businesses, crime incidents, or other spatial data.

- **Geospatial Time Series**: Combine spatial data with temporal elements to analyze changes over time. This can include animations that show how patterns evolve or transitions between different time periods.

5. Example Workflow for Geospatial Visualization

Here is a general workflow for creating a geospatial visualization:

1. **Prepare the Data**: Ensure the dataset includes geographic coordinates (latitude and longitude) or region identifiers. Clean and format the data as needed.

2. **Choose a Visualization Tool**: Select a tool or library based on the type of visualization you want to create and the features you need.

3. **Create the Visualization**: Use the chosen tool to plot the data on a map. Customize the map's appearance and interactivity according to your requirements.

4. **Analyze and Interpret**: Explore the map to identify patterns and insights. Use interactive features to drill down into specific areas or data points.

5. **Share and Communicate**: Present the visualization to stakeholders or include it in reports. Ensure that the visualization clearly communicates the intended message and findings.

6. Practical Applications

- **Urban Planning**: Analyzing land use, infrastructure, and population distribution to make decisions about zoning and development.

- **Public Health**: Tracking disease outbreaks, healthcare accessibility, and environmental factors affecting health.

- **Transportation and Logistics**: Optimizing routes, analyzing traffic patterns, and managing logistics based on geographic data.

- **Environmental Studies**: Monitoring environmental changes, such as deforestation, pollution, and climate impacts.

7. Conclusion

Geospatial data visualization is a powerful method for analyzing and presenting geographic information. By leveraging tools such as Geopandas, Folium, Plotly, and Mapbox, users can create detailed and interactive maps that reveal spatial patterns, relationships, and trends. Mastering these techniques enhances the ability to interpret geographic data and make informed decisions based on spatial insights.

Conceptual code examples for creating geospatial visualizations using different tools and libraries.

1. Geopandas: Choropleth Map

Concept: Visualize regional data with a choropleth map using Geopandas and Matplotlib.

```
import geopandas as gpd

import matplotlib.pyplot as plt


# Load a GeoDataFrame containing the geometry of the regions

world = gpd.read_file(gpd.datasets.get_path('naturalearth_lowres'))


# Assume we have a DataFrame with data to merge with the GeoDataFrame

data = {

    'continent': ['Asia', 'Europe', 'Africa', 'Oceania', 'North America', 'South America'],

    'population': [4457900000, 741400000, 1216000000, 43180000, 579000000, 422500000]

}

df = pd.DataFrame(data)


# Merge the DataFrame with the GeoDataFrame
```

```
world = world.merge(df, how='left', left_on='continent',
right_on='continent')


# Plot

fig, ax = plt.subplots(1, 1, figsize=(10, 6))

world.boundary.plot(ax=ax)

world.plot(column='population', ax=ax, legend=True,

        legend_kwds={'label': "Population by Continent",

                'orientation': "horizontal"})

plt.show()
```

2. Folium: Interactive Map with Markers

Concept: Create an interactive map with Folium, including markers for specific locations.

```
import folium


# Create a base map

m = folium.Map(location=[20,0], zoom_start=2)


# Add markers to the map

locations = [

    {"city": "New York", "lat": 40.7128, "lon": -74.0060},

    {"city": "London", "lat": 51.5074, "lon": -0.1278},

    {"city": "Tokyo", "lat": 35.6895, "lon": 139.6917}

]


for location in locations:
```

```
folium.Marker(
    location=[location["lat"], location["lon"]],
    popup=location["city"]
).add_to(m)


# Save to an HTML file
m.save('interactive_map.html')
```

3. Plotly: Scatter Plot on Map

Concept: Create a scatter plot on a map using Plotly for visualizing location data.

```
import plotly.express as px
import pandas as pd


# Create a DataFrame with location data
df = pd.DataFrame({
    'City': ['New York', 'London', 'Tokyo'],
    'Latitude': [40.7128, 51.5074, 35.6895],
    'Longitude': [-74.0060, -0.1278, 139.6917]
})


# Create the scatter plot map
fig = px.scatter_geo(df,
            lat='Latitude',
            lon='Longitude',
            text='City',
```

```
                    title='City Locations on Map')

fig.update_geos(projection_type="mercator")

fig.show()
```

4. Mapbox: Custom Map with Data

Concept: Use Mapbox to create a custom interactive map with data.

```python
import mapboxgl

from mapboxgl.viz import *

from mapboxgl.utils import create_color_stops

import pandas as pd


# Set Mapbox access token

mapboxgl.access_token = 'YOUR_MAPBOX_ACCESS_TOKEN'


# Create a DataFrame with data

df = pd.DataFrame({

    'lat': [40.7128, 51.5074, 35.6895],

    'lon': [-74.0060, -0.1278, 139.6917],

    'city': ['New York', 'London', 'Tokyo']

})


# Initialize a map

map_viz = CircleViz(df,

                access_token=mapboxgl.access_token,

                center=(-98.5795, 39.8283),
```

```
                 zoom=3,

                 radius=10,

                 color='city',

                 color_stops=create_color_stops(['New York', 'London',
'Tokyo'], ['red', 'blue', 'green']))


# Show map

map_viz.show()
```

5. Geospatial Time Series

Concept: Animate changes in spatial data over time.

```
import folium

import pandas as pd


# Data with time series and location information

data = pd.DataFrame({

    'time': ['2023-01-01', '2023-01-15', '2023-02-01'],

    'latitude': [40.7128, 40.7306, 40.7498],

    'longitude': [-74.0060, -73.9352, -73.9546],

    'location': ['Point A', 'Point B', 'Point C']

})


# Create a base map

m = folium.Map(location=[40.7128, -74.0060], zoom_start=12)


# Add time series markers
```

```
for _, row in data.iterrows():

    folium.Marker(

        location=[row['latitude'], row['longitude']],

        popup=f"{row['location']} on {row['time']}"

    ).add_to(m)


# Save to an HTML file

m.save('time_series_map.html')
```

These examples provide a starting point for creating various types of geospatial visualizations using different libraries and tools. You can customize these examples based on specific requirements and data.

Network Visualization

Concept: Network visualization involves representing complex networks, where nodes represent entities and edges represent relationships or interactions between these entities. This type of visualization helps to analyze and understand the structure and dynamics of networks, such as social networks, transportation systems, or biological networks.

Key Concepts

1. **Nodes and Edges**:

   o **Nodes**: Represent entities or objects in the network (e.g., people in a social network).

   o **Edges**: Represent connections or relationships between nodes (e.g., friendships or collaborations).

2. **Centrality Measures**:

   o **Degree Centrality**: The number of edges connected to a node. Nodes with high degree centrality are often considered important.

- o **Betweenness Centrality**: Measures how often a node lies on the shortest path between other nodes. Nodes with high betweenness centrality act as bridges.

- o **Closeness Centrality**: Indicates how close a node is to all other nodes in the network.

- o **Eigenvector Centrality**: Measures a node's influence based on the importance of its neighbors.

3. **Community Detection**: Identifying groups of nodes that are more densely connected with each other than with other nodes. Algorithms like Louvain or Girvan-Newman are often used for this purpose.

4. **Visualization Layouts**:

- o **Force-Directed Layouts**: Nodes are positioned using physical simulation algorithms, where edges act like springs and nodes repel each other.

- o **Circular Layouts**: Nodes are arranged in a circle, often used for simpler networks or when node positions are less important.

5. **Interactive Visualizations**: Enhancing network visualization with interactivity to explore and analyze the network dynamically.

Code Examples

1. Network Visualization with NetworkX and Matplotlib

NetworkX is a popular library for the creation, manipulation, and study of complex networks. Here's a basic example of visualizing a network:

```
import networkx as nx
import matplotlib.pyplot as plt


# Create a new graph
G = nx.Graph()
```

```
# Add nodes
G.add_nodes_from([1, 2, 3, 4, 5])


# Add edges
G.add_edges_from([(1, 2), (2, 3), (3, 4), (4, 5), (5, 1), (1, 3)])


# Draw the network
plt.figure(figsize=(8, 6))

nx.draw(G, with_labels=True, node_color='skyblue', node_size=700,
edge_color='gray', font_size=16)

plt.title('Simple Network Visualization')

plt.show()
```

2. Interactive Network Visualization with Plotly

Plotly can create interactive network visualizations that allow users to zoom, pan, and hover over nodes for additional information.

```
import plotly.graph_objects as go

import networkx as nx


# Create a new graph
G = nx.Graph()


# Add nodes
G.add_nodes_from([1, 2, 3, 4, 5])


# Add edges
G.add_edges_from([(1, 2), (2, 3), (3, 4), (4, 5), (5, 1), (1, 3)])
```

```python
# Extract node positions
pos = nx.spring_layout(G)


# Extract node and edge information
edge_x = []
edge_y = []
for edge in G.edges():
    x0, y0 = pos[edge[0]]
    x1, y1 = pos[edge[1]]
    edge_x.append(x0)
    edge_x.append(x1)
    edge_y.append(y0)
    edge_y.append(y1)


# Create the network visualization
fig = go.Figure()


# Add edges
fig.add_trace(go.Scatter(x=edge_x, y=edge_y, mode='lines',
line=dict(width=1, color='gray')))


# Add nodes
node_x = [pos[node][0] for node in G.nodes()]
node_y = [pos[node][1] for node in G.nodes()]
```

```
fig.add_trace(go.Scatter(x=node_x, y=node_y, mode='markers+text',
text=[str(node) for node in G.nodes()],
                    marker=dict(size=10, color='skyblue', line=dict(width=2,
color='black'))))


fig.update_layout(title='Interactive Network Visualization',
showlegend=False)
fig.show()
```

3. Network Visualization with Gephi

Gephi is a powerful tool for network analysis and visualization. It is used for larger and more complex networks where interactive exploration and analysis are required.

- **Data Preparation**: Export the network data from Python to a format suitable for Gephi, such as GEXF or CSV.

- **Visualization**: Load the data into Gephi, and use its various layout algorithms and tools to explore and analyze the network interactively.

Summary

Network visualization provides insights into the structure and dynamics of networks by displaying relationships between entities. Tools like NetworkX, Plotly, and Gephi help in visualizing, analyzing, and interacting with network data. Interactive visualizations enhance the ability to explore complex networks and uncover patterns or anomalies effectively.

Chapter 20: Time Series Analysis

Introduction to Time Series Data

Concept: Time series data consists of observations recorded sequentially over time. Unlike traditional datasets where observations are independent, time series data involves a temporal order where past values influence future values. This makes time series analysis essential for forecasting, anomaly detection, and understanding trends and seasonal patterns.

Key Concepts

1. **Definition of Time Series Data**:

   o **Time Series**: A series of data points indexed in time order. For example, daily stock prices, monthly rainfall, or hourly temperature readings.

   o **Timestamp**: The time at which each observation is recorded.

2. **Components of Time Series**:

   o **Trend**: The long-term movement in the data over time. It represents the general direction in which the data is moving.

   o **Seasonality**: Regular, periodic fluctuations occurring at consistent intervals, such as monthly or quarterly cycles.

   o **Noise**: Random variations or irregular fluctuations that cannot be attributed to trend or seasonality.

   o **Cyclic Patterns**: Fluctuations in the data that occur at irregular intervals, often related to economic or business cycles.

3. **Time Series Decomposition**:

   o **Decomposition**: Breaking down a time series into its trend, seasonal, and residual components. This helps in understanding the underlying patterns and improving forecasting accuracy.

4. **Stationarity**:

   o **Stationarity**: A time series is stationary if its statistical properties (mean, variance) do not change over time. Many time series models assume stationarity to simplify analysis and forecasting.

5. **Lag and Autocorrelation**:

   o **Lag**: The difference between the current time and a past time point in the series.

   o **Autocorrelation**: The correlation of a time series with its own past values. It helps to identify patterns and dependencies in the data.

Code Examples

1. Generating and Plotting Time Series Data

Below is an example of how to generate and visualize time series data using Python and libraries like pandas and matplotlib.

```python
import pandas as pd
import numpy as np
import matplotlib.pyplot as plt

# Generate a time series with a trend and seasonality
np.random.seed(0)
dates = pd.date_range(start='2020-01-01', periods=100, freq='D')
trend = np.linspace(0, 10, 100)
seasonal = 5 * np.sin(np.linspace(0, 10, 100))
noise = np.random.normal(0, 1, 100)
data = trend + seasonal + noise
```

```python
# Create a DataFrame
df = pd.DataFrame({'Date': dates, 'Value': data})
df.set_index('Date', inplace=True)

# Plot the time series
plt.figure(figsize=(12, 6))
plt.plot(df.index, df['Value'], label='Time Series Data')
plt.title('Generated Time Series Data')
plt.xlabel('Date')
plt.ylabel('Value')
plt.legend()
plt.show()
```

2. Decomposing Time Series Data

Using statsmodels, you can decompose the time series to analyze its components.

```python
from statsmodels.tsa.seasonal import seasonal_decompose

# Decompose the time series
decomposition = seasonal_decompose(df['Value'], model='additive')
trend = decomposition.trend
seasonal = decomposition.seasonal
residual = decomposition.resid

# Plot the decomposition
```

```python
plt.figure(figsize=(12, 10))


plt.subplot(4, 1, 1)
plt.plot(df.index, df['Value'], label='Original')
plt.title('Original Time Series')
plt.legend()


plt.subplot(4, 1, 2)
plt.plot(df.index, trend, label='Trend')
plt.title('Trend Component')
plt.legend()


plt.subplot(4, 1, 3)
plt.plot(df.index, seasonal, label='Seasonal')
plt.title('Seasonal Component')
plt.legend()


plt.subplot(4, 1, 4)
plt.plot(df.index, residual, label='Residual')
plt.title('Residual Component')
plt.legend()


plt.tight_layout()
plt.show()
```

3. Checking for Stationarity

Using the Augmented Dickey-Fuller (ADF) test to check for stationarity.

```
from statsmodels.tsa.stattools import adfuller

# Perform ADF test
result = adfuller(df['Value'].dropna())

print('ADF Statistic:', result[0])
print('p-value:', result[1])
print('Critical Values:', result[4])
```

- **ADF Statistic**: Value of the test statistic.

- **p-value**: Probability of observing the test statistic under the null hypothesis of non-stationarity.

- **Critical Values**: Thresholds for rejecting the null hypothesis.

Time series data involves observations recorded sequentially over time, making it crucial for forecasting and trend analysis. Key components include trend, seasonality, noise, and cyclic patterns. Decomposition helps to break down and understand these components, while stationarity is essential for many time series models. Tools like pandas, matplotlib, and statsmodels assist in generating, visualizing, and analyzing time series data.

Time Series Decomposition

Concept: Time series decomposition involves breaking down a time series into its fundamental components to better understand its structure. The primary components are trend, seasonality, and residuals.

Key Points:

- **Trend**: Represents the long-term movement or direction in the data. It shows the overall upward or downward trajectory over time.

- **Seasonality**: Refers to regular, periodic fluctuations that occur at consistent intervals, such as daily, monthly, or yearly cycles. Seasonal patterns are often influenced by external factors like weather or holidays.

- **Residuals**: The irregular, random fluctuations remaining after removing the trend and seasonal components. Residuals help identify anomalies and noise in the data.

Forecasting Techniques (e.g., ARIMA, Prophet)

Concept: Forecasting involves predicting future values of a time series based on its historical data. Various techniques are used depending on the nature of the data and the specific requirements of the forecasting task.

Key Points:

- **ARIMA (AutoRegressive Integrated Moving Average)**: A widely used statistical method for time series forecasting that combines autoregressive (AR) terms, differencing (I), and moving average (MA) terms. ARIMA models are suitable for stationary time series.

- **Prophet**: A forecasting tool developed by Facebook designed to handle time series data with strong seasonal effects and missing values. Prophet decomposes the time series into trend, seasonality, and holiday components to make forecasts.

Seasonality and Trend Analysis

Concept: Seasonality and trend analysis focuses on identifying and interpreting the periodic patterns and long-term movements in time series data.

Key Points:

- **Seasonality**: Regular and predictable patterns that repeat over specific intervals. Analyzing seasonality helps in understanding recurring events and cycles.

- **Trend Analysis**: Identifying the general direction of the data over a longer period. It helps in understanding the underlying growth or decline patterns and making informed projections.

Recommender Systems

Concept: Recommender systems are algorithms designed to suggest items to users based on their preferences and behaviors. They are widely used in e-commerce, streaming services, and social media platforms.

Key Points:

- **Collaborative Filtering**: This approach makes recommendations based on the behavior and preferences of similar users. It relies on user-item interactions and can be user-based or item-based.

- **Content-Based Filtering**: This method recommends items based on the attributes of the items and the user's preferences. It uses features of the items and user profiles to make recommendations.

- **Hybrid Recommender Systems**: Combine collaborative filtering and content-based filtering to leverage the strengths of both approaches and provide more accurate recommendations.

Anomaly Detection

Concept: Anomaly detection involves identifying unusual or unexpected patterns in data that do not conform to the norm. It is crucial for detecting fraud, equipment failures, and other rare events.

Key Points:

- **Understanding Anomalies**: Anomalies are data points that deviate significantly from the expected pattern. They can indicate errors, fraud, or significant changes in the system.

- **Statistical Methods**: Traditional methods involve statistical techniques like z-scores and statistical tests to detect anomalies based on historical distributions.

- **Machine Learning-Based Anomaly Detection**: Advanced techniques use machine learning models to identify anomalies by learning patterns from historical data and recognizing deviations.

Advanced Machine Learning Topics

Concept: Advanced machine learning topics encompass a range of sophisticated techniques and methodologies that build upon fundamental concepts to address complex problems.

Key Points:

- **Ensemble Methods**: Techniques like bagging and boosting combine multiple models to improve prediction accuracy and robustness. Beyond these, methods like stacking use meta-learning to combine the strengths of different models.

- **Bayesian Machine Learning**: This approach incorporates prior knowledge and probability distributions into the learning process. Bayesian methods are useful for uncertainty estimation and incorporating domain knowledge.

- **Meta-Learning and Model Stacking**: Meta-learning involves training models to learn how to learn, improving their performance across different tasks. Model stacking combines multiple models to leverage their individual strengths and improve overall performance.

- **Deep Reinforcement Learning**: Combines deep learning with reinforcement learning principles to enable agents to learn optimal behaviors through interactions with an environment.

Model Interpretability and Explainability

Concept: Model interpretability and explainability focus on understanding and explaining the decisions and predictions made by machine learning models.

Key Points:

- **Techniques for Interpreting Models**: Methods include feature importance, partial dependence plots, and SHAP (SHapley Additive exPlanations) values. These techniques help understand which features influence predictions and how.

- **Feature Importance**: Measures the impact of each feature on the model's predictions, helping to identify key factors and improve model transparency.

- **Model-Agnostic Methods**: Techniques that can be applied to any machine learning model, regardless of its underlying architecture, to provide explanations and insights.

- **Case Studies on Interpretability**: Real-world examples demonstrate how model interpretability is used to build trust, meet regulatory requirements, and improve decision-making.

Practical Applications of Machine Learning

Concept: Practical applications of machine learning involve deploying and using machine learning models in real-world scenarios across various industries.

Key Points:

- **Real-World Case Studies**: Examples from industries like finance, healthcare, and retail illustrate how machine learning is applied to solve specific problems and drive business value.

- **Applications in Different Industries**: Machine learning techniques are used for fraud detection, predictive maintenance, personalized recommendations, and more.

- **Challenges and Considerations**: Issues include data quality, model deployment, scalability, and integration with existing systems. Addressing these challenges is crucial for successful implementation.

- **Ethical Implications and Responsible AI Practices**: Ensuring that machine learning models are used ethically, avoiding bias, and adhering to responsible AI practices are essential for maintaining trust and fairness.

This discussion provides a foundation for understanding the key topics in time series analysis, recommender systems, anomaly detection, advanced machine learning methods, model interpretability, and practical applications of machine learning.

Time Series Decomposition

Concept: Time series decomposition is a method used to break down a time series into its underlying components to better understand its structure and make forecasting easier. The main goal of decomposition is to separate the time series into its constituent parts: trend, seasonality, and residuals.

Key Components

1. **Trend**:
   - o **Definition**: The trend represents the long-term movement or direction in the data. It shows the overall trajectory of the time series over an extended period, indicating whether the values are generally increasing, decreasing, or remaining stable.
   - o **Concept**: Identifying the trend helps in understanding the general direction of the data, which is crucial for making long-term forecasts. Trends can be linear or nonlinear, and they are often driven by factors such as economic growth, technological advancements, or demographic changes.

2. **Seasonality**:
   - o **Definition**: Seasonality refers to regular, repeating patterns in the data that occur at consistent intervals, such as daily, monthly, or yearly. These patterns are usually influenced by external factors like weather, holidays, or events.
   - o **Concept**: Seasonality is important for understanding periodic fluctuations in the data. For example, retail sales often peak during holiday seasons, and electricity consumption might rise during summer months. Recognizing and accounting for seasonality helps in creating more accurate forecasts.

3. **Residuals**:
   - o **Definition**: Residuals are the remaining variations in the time series after removing the trend and seasonal components. They represent the noise or random fluctuations that cannot be explained by the trend or seasonality.
   - o **Concept**: Analyzing residuals is crucial for diagnosing the quality of the decomposition and identifying any anomalies or irregular patterns. Residuals should ideally resemble white noise, meaning they should be random and uncorrelated.

Decomposition Methods

1. **Additive Decomposition**:

   o **Concept**: In additive decomposition, the time series is assumed to be the sum of its components: $Y(t)=T(t) + S(t) + R(t)$, where $Y(t)$ is the observed value at time t, $T(t)$ is the trend component, $S(t)$ is the seasonal component, and $R(t)$ is the residual component.

   o **Use Case**: Additive decomposition is appropriate when the magnitude of seasonal fluctuations and trend changes are relatively constant over time.

2. **Multiplicative Decomposition**:

   o **Concept**: In multiplicative decomposition, the time series is assumed to be the product of its components: $Y(t) = T(t) \times S(t) \times R(t)$. This approach is used when the seasonal variations change proportionally with the level of the trend.

   o **Use Case**: Multiplicative decomposition is suitable when the amplitude of seasonal fluctuations grows or shrinks with the trend.

Practical Application

- **Process**:

  1. **Model Selection**: Choose between additive or multiplicative decomposition based on the nature of the data.

  2. **Decomposition**: Use statistical methods or software tools to separate the time series into trend, seasonal, and residual components.

  3. **Analysis**: Examine each component to understand the underlying patterns and refine the forecasting model accordingly.

- **Tools**: Many data analysis libraries and tools provide functions for time series decomposition. For example, the seasonal_decompose function in Python's statsmodels library can perform both additive and multiplicative decomposition.

Example (Conceptual Overview)

1. **Original Time Series**: Consider a time series representing monthly sales data.

2. **Decomposition**:

   o **Trend Component**: A line showing the overall upward or downward trend in sales over the years.

   o **Seasonal Component**: A repeating pattern reflecting increased sales during the holiday season.

   o **Residual Component**: Random variations or anomalies not explained by the trend or seasonality.

By decomposing a time series into these components, you can gain insights into the underlying patterns and better understand the factors influencing the data. This understanding can help in creating more accurate forecasts and making informed business decisions.

Here are code examples for time series decomposition using Python, illustrating both additive and multiplicative decomposition. We will use the statsmodels library for this purpose.

Code Example: Time Series Decomposition

Import Libraries

```
import pandas as pd

import numpy as np

import matplotlib.pyplot as plt

from statsmodels.tsa.seasonal import seasonal_decompose


# Generate a sample time series data

np.random.seed(0)
```

```
dates = pd.date_range(start='2021-01-01', periods=100, freq='M')

data = pd.Series(np.random.randn(100) * 10 + np.linspace(0, 50, 100),
index=dates)


# Add seasonality

seasonal_pattern = np.sin(np.linspace(0, 2 * np.pi, 12))

seasonal_data = np.tile(seasonal_pattern, 100 // 12 + 1)[:100] * 5

data += seasonal_data
```

Additive Decomposition

```
# Perform additive decomposition

result_additive = seasonal_decompose(data, model='additive')


# Plot the components

plt.figure(figsize=(12, 8))

plt.subplot(4, 1, 1)

plt.plot(result_additive.observed, label='Observed')

plt.title('Additive Decomposition')

plt.legend()


plt.subplot(4, 1, 2)

plt.plot(result_additive.trend, label='Trend')

plt.legend()


plt.subplot(4, 1, 3)

plt.plot(result_additive.seasonal, label='Seasonal')
```

```
plt.legend()

plt.subplot(4, 1, 4)
plt.plot(result_additive.resid, label='Residual')
plt.legend()

plt.tight_layout()
plt.show()
```

Multiplicative Decomposition

```
# Perform multiplicative decomposition
result_multiplicative = seasonal_decompose(data, model='multiplicative')

# Plot the components
plt.figure(figsize=(12, 8))
plt.subplot(4, 1, 1)
plt.plot(result_multiplicative.observed, label='Observed')
plt.title('Multiplicative Decomposition')
plt.legend()

plt.subplot(4, 1, 2)
plt.plot(result_multiplicative.trend, label='Trend')
plt.legend()

plt.subplot(4, 1, 3)
plt.plot(result_multiplicative.seasonal, label='Seasonal')
```

```
plt.legend()


plt.subplot(4, 1, 4)

plt.plot(result_multiplicative.resid, label='Residual')

plt.legend()


plt.tight_layout()

plt.show()
```

Explanation

- **Import Libraries**: Import necessary libraries and generate sample time series data with a trend and seasonality.

- **Additive Decomposition**: Apply additive decomposition to the time series using seasonal_decompose with the model set to 'additive'. Plot the observed data, trend, seasonal, and residual components.

- **Multiplicative Decomposition**: Apply multiplicative decomposition using the same function but with the model set to 'multiplicative'. Plot the results similarly to compare with the additive decomposition.

These code examples illustrate how to decompose a time series into its components and visualize them. By examining the individual components, you can better understand the underlying patterns and make more informed decisions based on the data.

Forecasting Techniques: ARIMA and Prophet

ARIMA (AutoRegressive Integrated Moving Average)

ARIMA is a widely used statistical model for time series forecasting. It combines three components:

1. **AutoRegressive (AR) Term**: This component captures the relationship between an observation and a number of lagged observations.

2. **Integrated (I) Term**: This component represents the differencing of raw observations to make the time series stationary.

3. **Moving Average (MA) Term**: This component captures the relationship between an observation and a residual error from a moving average model applied to lagged observations.

The ARIMA model is parameterized by three terms: (p,d,q), where:

- p is the number of lag observations included in the model (AR term).

- d is the number of times that the raw observations are differenced (I term).

- q is the size of the moving average window (MA term).

Example: ARIMA Forecasting

Here's a step-by-step guide to applying ARIMA using Python:

```python
import pandas as pd

import numpy as np

import matplotlib.pyplot as plt

from statsmodels.tsa.arima_model import ARIMA

from statsmodels.tsa.seasonal import seasonal_decompose


# Generate sample time series data

np.random.seed(0)

dates = pd.date_range(start='2021-01-01', periods=100, freq='M')

data = pd.Series(np.random.randn(100) * 10 + np.linspace(0, 50, 100),
index=dates)
```

```python
# Add seasonality
seasonal_pattern = np.sin(np.linspace(0, 2 * np.pi, 12))
seasonal_data = np.tile(seasonal_pattern, 100 // 12 + 1)[:100] * 5
data += seasonal_data


# Decompose the time series
result = seasonal_decompose(data, model='additive')
data_detrended = data - result.trend

# Fit ARIMA model
model = ARIMA(data_detrended.dropna(), order=(5, 1, 0))  # Example
order (p,d,q)
model_fit = model.fit(disp=0)


# Forecast
forecast = model_fit.forecast(steps=12)
forecast_index = pd.date_range(start=data.index[-1] + pd.DateOffset(1),
periods=12, freq='M')
forecast_series = pd.Series(forecast[0], index=forecast_index)


# Plot results
plt.figure(figsize=(12, 6))
plt.plot(data, label='Original Data')
plt.plot(forecast_series, color='red', linestyle='--', label='Forecast')
plt.title('ARIMA Forecasting')
plt.legend()
```

```
plt.show()
```

Prophet

Prophet is a forecasting tool developed by Facebook that is specifically designed for forecasting time series with daily observations that display patterns on different time scales (e.g., yearly, weekly). It is particularly useful for time series with strong seasonal effects and several seasons of historical data.

Key Components of Prophet:

1. **Trend**: A piecewise linear or logistic growth trend.

2. **Seasonality**: Both yearly and weekly seasonality, with the option to add custom seasonalities.

3. **Holidays**: Incorporates effects of holidays or special events that might affect the time series.

Example: Prophet Forecasting

Here's how you can use Prophet to forecast time series data:

```python
import pandas as pd

import numpy as np

import matplotlib.pyplot as plt

from fbprophet import Prophet


# Generate sample time series data

np.random.seed(0)

dates = pd.date_range(start='2021-01-01', periods=100, freq='M')

data = pd.Series(np.random.randn(100) * 10 + np.linspace(0, 50, 100), index=dates)


# Add seasonality
```

```python
seasonal_pattern = np.sin(np.linspace(0, 2 * np.pi, 12))
seasonal_data = np.tile(seasonal_pattern, 100 // 12 + 1)[:100] * 5
data += seasonal_data

# Prepare data for Prophet
df = pd.DataFrame({'ds': data.index, 'y': data.values})

# Initialize and fit Prophet model
model = Prophet(yearly_seasonality=True, weekly_seasonality=True)
model.fit(df)

# Create future dataframe
future = model.make_future_dataframe(periods=12, freq='M')
forecast = model.predict(future)

# Plot results
fig = model.plot(forecast)
plt.title('Prophet Forecasting')
plt.show()
```

Conceptual Discussion

- **ARIMA**: Suitable for time series data with clear trends and seasonality. It requires the data to be stationary, which means that statistical properties like mean and variance do not change over time. ARIMA models are quite flexible and can model a wide range of time series patterns by adjusting the parameters p, d, and q.

- **Prophet**: Designed to handle more complex time series data with multiple seasonal effects and large amounts of historical data. Prophet's ability to include holidays and special events makes it more versatile for practical business applications. It is particularly useful for data with strong yearly or weekly patterns and is robust to missing data.

Both ARIMA and Prophet offer powerful forecasting capabilities, and the choice between them depends on the nature of your time series data and the specific requirements of your forecasting task.

Seasonality and Trend Analysis

Understanding Seasonality and Trends

Seasonality and **trend** are two crucial components of time series data that help in understanding and forecasting patterns over time.

1. **Trend**: A trend refers to the long-term movement or direction in a time series. It can be an upward or downward trajectory over a longer period, indicating general shifts in data over time. Trends are usually identified by looking at the overall direction of the data.

2. **Seasonality**: Seasonality refers to regular, repeating patterns or fluctuations in a time series that occur at specific intervals, such as daily, weekly, monthly, or yearly. These patterns are often driven by external factors like holidays, seasons, or other periodic events.

Decomposition of Time Series

Time series decomposition is a technique used to separate the time series data into its underlying components: trend, seasonality, and residuals. This helps in understanding the behavior of the data and in making more accurate forecasts.

Methods for Decomposition

1. **Additive Decomposition**: Assumes that the time series can be represented as the sum of trend, seasonality, and residuals:

$$Y_t = T_t + S_t + R_t$$

where Y_t is the observed data, T_t is the trend component, S_t is the seasonal component, and R_t is the residual component.

2. **Multiplicative Decomposition**: Assumes that the time series can be represented as the product of trend, seasonality, and residuals:

$$Y_t = T_t x S_t x R_t$$

This method is useful when the seasonal variations increase or decrease proportionally with the level of the trend.

Example: Seasonality and Trend Analysis with Python

Here's how you can perform seasonality and trend analysis using Python, specifically with the statsmodels library for decomposition:

```python
import pandas as pd

import numpy as np

import matplotlib.pyplot as plt

from statsmodels.tsa.seasonal import seasonal_decompose


# Generate sample time series data

np.random.seed(0)

dates = pd.date_range(start='2021-01-01', periods=100, freq='M')

data = pd.Series(np.random.randn(100) * 10 + np.linspace(0, 50, 100),
index=dates)


# Add seasonality

seasonal_pattern = np.sin(np.linspace(0, 2 * np.pi, 12))

seasonal_data = np.tile(seasonal_pattern, 100 // 12 + 1)[:100] * 5

data += seasonal_data
```

```python
# Decompose the time series
result = seasonal_decompose(data, model='additive')  # Use
model='multiplicative' for multiplicative decomposition


# Extract components
trend = result.trend
seasonal = result.seasonal
residual = result.resid


# Plot results
plt.figure(figsize=(14, 8))
plt.subplot(4, 1, 1)
plt.plot(data, label='Original Data')
plt.title('Original Data')


plt.subplot(4, 1, 2)
plt.plot(trend, label='Trend', color='orange')
plt.title('Trend Component')


plt.subplot(4, 1, 3)
plt.plot(seasonal, label='Seasonal', color='green')
plt.title('Seasonal Component')


plt.subplot(4, 1, 4)
plt.plot(residual, label='Residual', color='red')
```

```
plt.title('Residual Component')

plt.tight_layout()
plt.show()
```

Key Concepts

- **Trend Analysis**: Involves identifying and quantifying the general direction in the data. This can be achieved through methods like moving averages or polynomial fitting. Trends are essential for understanding the overall direction of the data.

- **Seasonality Analysis**: Focuses on detecting and quantifying repeating patterns within a fixed period. This involves methods like Fourier analysis or seasonal decomposition. Seasonality often requires identifying the appropriate periodicity (e.g., monthly, quarterly) for accurate modeling.

Practical Tips

1. **Visual Inspection**: Always start with visualizing the time series data to get a sense of trends and seasonal patterns.

2. **Stationarity**: Ensure the time series data is stationary before applying certain forecasting methods, as trends and seasonality can affect stationarity.

3. **Model Selection**: Choose the decomposition model (additive vs. multiplicative) based on the nature of the data. If seasonal variations change proportionally with the trend, a multiplicative model may be more appropriate.

By understanding and analyzing seasonality and trends, you can gain valuable insights into the time series data and make more informed forecasting decisions.

Chapter 21: Recommender Systems

Introduction to Recommender Systems

Recommender systems are algorithms designed to suggest products, services, or information to users based on various factors, including their preferences, behaviors, and interactions. These systems are prevalent in many online platforms, such as e-commerce sites, streaming services, and social media, where they enhance user experience by providing personalized recommendations.

Types of Recommender Systems

Recommender systems generally fall into three main categories:

1. **Collaborative Filtering**: This approach relies on user interactions and preferences to make recommendations. It operates under the assumption that users who have similar preferences in the past will have similar preferences in the future. Collaborative filtering can be further classified into:

    o **User-Based Collaborative Filtering**: This method recommends items by finding users with similar preferences and suggesting items they liked.

    o **Item-Based Collaborative Filtering**: This method recommends items similar to those that a user has liked or interacted with in the past. It looks at the relationships between items rather than users.

2. **Content-Based Filtering**: This approach uses the characteristics of items to recommend similar items based on the user's previous interactions and preferences. For example, if a user likes a particular genre of movies, the system will suggest other movies in the same genre. Content-based filtering requires detailed information about the items and user preferences.

3. **Hybrid Recommender Systems**: Hybrid systems combine collaborative filtering and content-based filtering methods to leverage the strengths of both approaches. They aim to provide

more accurate and diverse recommendations by integrating multiple sources of information.

Key Concepts and Techniques

1. **Similarity Measures**: To make recommendations, recommender systems use various similarity measures to quantify how similar items or users are to one another. Common similarity measures include cosine similarity, Pearson correlation, and Jaccard index.

2. **Matrix Factorization**: This technique is often used in collaborative filtering to reduce the dimensionality of user-item interaction matrices. By decomposing the matrix into lower-dimensional matrices, it helps in capturing latent factors that explain user preferences and item characteristics. Popular methods include Singular Value Decomposition (SVD) and Alternating Least Squares (ALS).

3. **Neighborhood Methods**: These methods involve finding a subset of similar users or items (the "neighborhood") and using their preferences to make recommendations. For user-based collaborative filtering, the neighborhood consists of users with similar preferences. For item-based filtering, it consists of items similar to the ones the user likes.

4. **Evaluation Metrics**: Recommender systems are evaluated using metrics such as Precision, Recall, F1 Score, Mean Absolute Error (MAE), and Root Mean Square Error (RMSE). These metrics help in assessing the quality and accuracy of recommendations.

Applications of Recommender Systems

Recommender systems are widely used across various domains:

- **E-commerce**: Recommending products based on past purchases, browsing history, and user preferences.

- **Streaming Services**: Suggesting movies, TV shows, or music based on viewing or listening history.

- **Social Media**: Recommending friends, groups, or content based on user interactions and interests.

- **News and Articles**: Personalizing news feeds and article recommendations based on user reading history.

Challenges and Considerations

1. **Cold Start Problem**: Recommender systems face challenges when dealing with new users or items with limited data. Techniques such as hybrid approaches or incorporating metadata can help address this issue.

2. **Scalability**: As the number of users and items grows, the recommender system must handle large-scale data efficiently. Techniques such as matrix factorization and scalable algorithms are essential for managing large datasets.

3. **Diversity and Serendipity**: Ensuring that recommendations are not only relevant but also diverse and unexpected can improve user satisfaction and engagement. Balancing relevance with diversity is a key consideration in designing effective recommender systems.

4. **Privacy and Ethics**: Recommender systems often rely on user data to provide personalized recommendations. It's crucial to handle user data responsibly and address privacy concerns. Implementing transparent data practices and ensuring user consent are important for ethical recommendations.

Recommender systems play a vital role in enhancing user experience by providing personalized recommendations. Understanding the different types of recommender systems, key concepts, and challenges helps in designing and implementing effective systems that meet user needs and preferences. By leveraging collaborative filtering, content-based filtering, and hybrid approaches, businesses can offer valuable and engaging recommendations that drive user satisfaction and engagement.

Example Code for Collaborative Filtering

Here's a basic example of how to implement user-based collaborative filtering using Python and the surprise library:

```
from surprise import Dataset, Reader

from surprise import KNNBasic

from surprise import accuracy
```

```python
from surprise.model_selection import train_test_split

# Load dataset
data = Dataset.load_builtin('ml-100k')
reader = Reader(line_format='user item rating timestamp', sep='\t')
data = Dataset.load_from_file('data/u.data', reader=reader)

# Split dataset into training and test sets
trainset, testset = train_test_split(data, test_size=0.25)

# Define the similarity options
sim_options = {
    'name': 'cosine',
    'user_based': True  # Compute similarities between users
}

# Build the model
model = KNNBasic(sim_options=sim_options)
model.fit(trainset)

# Make predictions
predictions = model.test(testset)

# Evaluate the model
accuracy.rmse(predictions)
```

In this example, the surprise library is used to load a dataset, split it into training and test sets, build a user-based collaborative filtering model, and evaluate its performance using root mean square error (RMSE).

Recommender systems are essential for providing personalized experiences in various domains. Understanding the different types of recommender systems, key concepts, and techniques helps in designing effective systems that cater to user preferences and enhance engagement. By leveraging collaborative filtering, content-based filtering, and hybrid approaches, businesses can deliver valuable recommendations and improve user satisfaction.

Item-Based Collaborative Filtering

Item-based collaborative filtering focuses on the similarity between items rather than users. It recommends items similar to those that the user has liked or interacted with. This method can be more scalable than user-based methods, especially in systems with a large number of users.

- **Similarity Measures**: Similarity between items is typically computed using:

  - **Cosine Similarity**: Measures the cosine of the angle between item vectors.

  - **Pearson Correlation**: Measures the linear correlation between the ratings of two items.

  - **Jaccard Index**: Measures the similarity between the sets of users who have interacted with the items.

- **Example Code**: Here's an example of item-based collaborative filtering using the surprise library:

```
from surprise import Dataset, Reader

from surprise import KNNBasic

from surprise import accuracy
```

```python
from surprise.model_selection import train_test_split

# Load dataset
data = Dataset.load_builtin('ml-100k')
reader = Reader(line_format='user item rating timestamp', sep='\t')
data = Dataset.load_from_file('data/u.data', reader=reader)

# Split dataset into training and test sets
trainset, testset = train_test_split(data, test_size=0.25)

# Define the similarity options
sim_options = {
    'name': 'cosine',
    'user_based': False  # Compute similarities between items
}

# Build the model
model = KNNBasic(sim_options=sim_options)
model.fit(trainset)

# Make predictions
predictions = model.test(testset)

# Evaluate the model
accuracy.rmse(predictions)
```

Challenges and Considerations

1. Scalability

Collaborative filtering methods can be computationally expensive, especially with large datasets. User-based methods may struggle with scalability as the number of users grows. Item-based methods are often preferred in such cases due to their better scalability.

2. Sparsity

The user-item interaction matrix in collaborative filtering is often sparse, meaning that most of the entries are missing. This sparsity can make it difficult to find similar users or items and may affect the quality of recommendations.

3. Cold Start Problem

The cold start problem occurs when the system has insufficient data about new users or items. Collaborative filtering relies on historical interactions, so new users or items without sufficient data may not receive accurate recommendations.

4. Overfitting

Collaborative filtering models can sometimes overfit to the training data, leading to poor generalization on unseen data. Regularization techniques and model evaluation strategies can help mitigate overfitting.

Collaborative filtering is a fundamental technique in recommender systems that leverages user behavior and preferences to make personalized recommendations. By using user-based or item-based approaches, collaborative filtering can provide valuable suggestions based on the preferences of similar users or items. Despite its challenges, collaborative filtering remains a powerful tool for enhancing user experience and engagement in various applications.

Here's an example of how to implement content-based filtering using Python. In this example, we'll use a simple dataset of movies with attributes and a user profile to generate recommendations.

```python
import pandas as pd

from sklearn.feature_extraction.text import TfidfVectorizer

from sklearn.metrics.pairwise import cosine_similarity


# Sample data: movies with genres as attributes
movies = pd.DataFrame({
    'movie_id': [1, 2, 3, 4, 5],
    'title': ['Movie A', 'Movie B', 'Movie C', 'Movie D', 'Movie E'],
    'genres': ['Action|Adventure', 'Action|Sci-Fi', 'Adventure|Fantasy',
'Drama|Romance', 'Sci-Fi|Thriller']
})


# User profile: prefers Action and Sci-Fi genres
user_profile = 'Action|Sci-Fi'


# Convert genres to TF-IDF vectors
vectorizer = TfidfVectorizer()

tfidf_matrix = vectorizer.fit_transform(movies['genres'])

user_vector = vectorizer.transform([user_profile])


# Compute similarity scores
similarity_scores = cosine_similarity(user_vector, tfidf_matrix)
```

```
# Add similarity scores to movies DataFrame

movies['similarity'] = similarity_scores.flatten()


# Sort movies by similarity scores

recommended_movies = movies.sort_values(by='similarity',
ascending=False)


# Print recommended movies

print("Recommended Movies:")

print(recommended_movies[['title', 'similarity']])
```

Explanation

1. **Data Preparation**: The dataset includes movie titles and their genres. Genres are treated as the features of items.

2. **User Profile**: A user profile is created with genres that the user prefers.

3. **TF-IDF Vectorization**: The TfidfVectorizer converts genre descriptions into numerical vectors. This representation captures the importance of each genre term in the dataset.

4. **Similarity Calculation**: Cosine similarity is used to measure how similar each movie's genre vector is to the user profile vector.

5. **Recommendation Generation**: Movies are sorted based on their similarity scores, and the top recommendations are presented to the user.

Advantages and Limitations

Advantages:

- **Personalization**: Recommendations are tailored to individual user preferences based on item attributes.

- **Independence**: Does not rely on other users' data, which is useful in systems with limited user interactions (cold start problem).

Limitations:

- **Limited Scope**: Recommendations are based solely on item features and may miss context or novelty.

- **Over-Specialization**: May recommend items that are too similar to those already known, limiting diversity in recommendations.

Content-based filtering is a powerful method for recommending items based on their features and user preferences. By focusing on item attributes and user profiles, content-based systems can provide relevant and personalized recommendations. However, it is important to balance content-based recommendations with other techniques to ensure diversity and novelty in the recommendation process.

Hybrid Recommender Systems

Hybrid recommender systems combine multiple recommendation techniques to leverage their strengths and mitigate their weaknesses. By integrating various methods, hybrid systems aim to improve recommendation accuracy, overcome limitations of individual approaches, and provide more diverse and relevant recommendations.

Key Concepts in Hybrid Recommender Systems

1. **Combination of Methods**

Hybrid recommender systems typically blend two or more of the following recommendation approaches:

- **Collaborative Filtering**: Uses user interactions and similarities to recommend items.

- **Content-Based Filtering**: Utilizes item attributes and user preferences to make recommendations.

- **Knowledge-Based Systems**: Relies on explicit knowledge or rules about users and items.

o **Demographic Filtering**: Uses demographic information to make recommendations based on user profiles.

2. **Hybrid Approaches**

Several strategies can be employed to combine different recommendation methods:

o **Weighted Hybrid**: Combines recommendations from multiple methods by assigning weights to each method and aggregating the results.

o **Switching Hybrid**: Chooses between different methods based on specific conditions, such as using content-based filtering when user data is scarce.

o **Mixed Hybrid**: Provides recommendations from multiple methods simultaneously and presents them together.

o **Cascade Hybrid**: Applies one recommendation method first and then uses another method to refine the results.

3. **Advantages of Hybrid Systems**

o **Enhanced Accuracy**: By combining different methods, hybrid systems can provide more accurate and relevant recommendations.

o **Diverse Recommendations**: Hybrid approaches can offer a more diverse set of recommendations by integrating different perspectives.

o **Reduced Cold Start Problem**: By leveraging various methods, hybrid systems can address the cold start problem (difficulty in making recommendations for new users or items) more effectively.

4. **Implementation Example**

Here's an example of a simple hybrid recommender system that combines collaborative filtering and content-based filtering. We will use collaborative filtering to generate initial recommendations and then refine these recommendations using content-based filtering.

```python
import pandas as pd
from sklearn.feature_extraction.text import TfidfVectorizer
from sklearn.metrics.pairwise import cosine_similarity
from sklearn.neighbors import NearestNeighbors


# Sample data: movies with genres and user ratings
movies = pd.DataFrame({
    'movie_id': [1, 2, 3, 4, 5],
    'title': ['Movie A', 'Movie B', 'Movie C', 'Movie D', 'Movie E'],
    'genres': ['Action|Adventure', 'Action|Sci-Fi', 'Adventure|Fantasy',
'Drama|Romance', 'Sci-Fi|Thriller'],
    'ratings': [5, 4, 3, 2, 4]  # User ratings for simplicity
})


# User preferences for collaborative filtering (e.g., ratings)
user_ratings = pd.Series([5, 4, 3, 2, 4], index=[1, 2, 3, 4, 5])


# Collaborative Filtering: Nearest Neighbors to find similar items
nn = NearestNeighbors(n_neighbors=3)
ratings_matrix = movies[['ratings']].values
nn.fit(ratings_matrix)
distances, indices = nn.kneighbors(ratings_matrix)


# Content-Based Filtering: Use TF-IDF to match item genres
vectorizer = TfidfVectorizer()
```

```
tfidf_matrix = vectorizer.fit_transform(movies['genres'])

user_profile = vectorizer.transform(['Action|Sci-Fi'])


# Compute similarity scores for content-based filtering

similarity_scores = cosine_similarity(user_profile, tfidf_matrix)


# Generate content-based recommendations

movies['content_similarity'] = similarity_scores.flatten()


# Combine recommendations from both methods

movies['collab_similarity'] = [1 / d for d in distances[:, 1]]  # Inverse
distance as similarity

movies['final_score'] = (movies['collab_similarity'] +
movies['content_similarity']) / 2


# Sort movies by final score

recommended_movies = movies.sort_values(by='final_score',
ascending=False)


# Print recommended movies

print("Hybrid Recommended Movies:")

print(recommended_movies[['title', 'final_score']])
```

Explanation

1. **Data Preparation**: The dataset includes movie titles, genres, and user ratings.

2. **Collaborative Filtering**: Uses Nearest Neighbors to find similar items based on user ratings.

3. **Content-Based Filtering**: Uses TF-IDF to compute similarity scores between user preferences and item genres.

4. **Combining Results**: Scores from both collaborative filtering and content-based filtering are combined to generate final recommendations.

5. **Final Recommendations**: The final recommendations are sorted based on the combined score.

Advantages and Limitations

Advantages:

- **Comprehensive Recommendations**: By leveraging multiple methods, hybrid systems offer a more complete recommendation approach.

- **Improved Performance**: Combining different methods often leads to better performance compared to individual methods.

- **Flexibility**: Hybrid systems can be customized to fit specific needs and contexts.

Limitations:

- **Complexity**: Hybrid systems can be more complex to implement and tune compared to single-method systems.

- **Computational Cost**: Combining multiple methods may require more computational resources and time.

Hybrid recommender systems provide a powerful approach to delivering accurate and diverse recommendations by integrating various recommendation techniques. By combining collaborative filtering, content-based filtering, and other methods, hybrid systems can address the limitations of individual approaches and enhance the overall recommendation quality.

Chapter 22: Anomaly Detection

Anomaly detection is a crucial aspect of data analysis and machine learning that focuses on identifying unusual or unexpected patterns within a dataset. These anomalies, often referred to as outliers or deviations, can provide valuable insights into underlying issues, fraud, or other significant events. This chapter will cover the foundational concepts, methods, and applications of anomaly detection.

1. Understanding Anomalies

Definition and Types of Anomalies:

- **Anomalies**: Observations that deviate significantly from the majority of the data. They may indicate critical information, such as system faults, fraud, or novel patterns.

- **Types of Anomalies**:

    o **Point Anomalies**: Single data points that are significantly different from the rest (e.g., an unusual transaction amount).

    o **Contextual Anomalies**: Data points that are anomalous in a specific context (e.g., an unusually high temperature in winter).

    o **Collective Anomalies**: A set of data points that together form an anomaly (e.g., a sudden spike in network traffic).

2. Statistical Methods for Anomaly Detection

Statistical Approaches:

- **Z-Score**: Measures how many standard deviations an observation is from the mean. Points with a high absolute Z-score are considered anomalies.

- **Modified Z-Score**: An adjustment to the Z-score for datasets with non-normal distributions. It is less sensitive to outliers.

- **Box Plot Analysis**: Uses the interquartile range (IQR) to identify points that fall below or above certain thresholds, marking them as anomalies.

Key Concepts:

- **Assumptions**: Statistical methods often assume a specific distribution (e.g., normal distribution). If data deviates significantly from these assumptions, the methods may not perform well.

- **Thresholds**: Determining thresholds for anomaly detection involves balancing false positives (normal points flagged as anomalies) and false negatives (anomalies missed).

3. Machine Learning-Based Anomaly Detection

Algorithms and Techniques:

- **Isolation Forest**: An ensemble method that isolates anomalies by randomly selecting features and splitting data points. Anomalies are isolated more quickly than normal observations.

- **One-Class SVM**: A support vector machine designed to identify the boundary of the majority class and flag points outside this boundary as anomalies.

- **Autoencoders**: Neural networks trained to reconstruct input data. Anomalies are identified by the reconstruction error—higher errors suggest anomalies.

Key Concepts:

- **Feature Engineering**: The performance of machine learning methods often depends on the quality of features used. Proper feature selection and extraction are crucial.

- **Model Training**: Supervised anomaly detection requires labeled data for training, while unsupervised methods do not. Proper validation and testing are necessary to ensure effectiveness.

4. Application of Anomaly Detection

Real-World Use Cases:

- **Fraud Detection**: Identifying unusual transactions in financial systems that may indicate fraudulent activities.

- **Network Security**: Detecting irregular patterns in network traffic that could signify security breaches or cyber-attacks.

- **Industrial Monitoring**: Recognizing anomalies in machinery or equipment that may indicate malfunctions or wear.

Challenges:

- **Scalability**: Handling large volumes of data and ensuring that the anomaly detection system performs efficiently.

- **Dynamic Environments**: Adapting to changes in data patterns over time, such as evolving fraud schemes or shifting normal behavior.

Anomaly detection is a powerful tool for identifying unusual patterns in data that may signal critical issues or novel phenomena. By employing statistical methods or machine learning techniques, organizations can effectively detect and respond to anomalies across various domains, including finance, security, and industrial monitoring. Understanding the different types of anomalies, methods for detection, and practical applications helps in designing robust anomaly detection systems that provide actionable insights and enhance decision-making processes.

Statistical Methods for Anomaly Detection

Statistical methods for anomaly detection rely on the principles of statistical theory to identify data points that significantly deviate from the expected patterns in a dataset. These methods are particularly useful in scenarios where the data follows a known distribution or where statistical properties can be leveraged to detect deviations. This section explores some of the key statistical methods used for anomaly detection.

1. Z-Score Method

Z-Score measures how many standard deviations a data point is from the mean. In the Z-Score method, anomalies are identified based on how far they deviate from the mean of the dataset.

Concept:

- The Z-Score for a data point is calculated using the formula:

$$Z = \frac{X - \mu}{\sigma}$$

where X is the data point, μ is the mean of the dataset, and σ is the standard deviation.

Anomaly Detection:

- A common threshold for identifying anomalies is a Z-Score greater than 3 or less than -3, indicating that the data point is more than three standard deviations away from the mean.

Code Example (Python):

```python
import numpy as np
import pandas as pd

# Sample data
data = pd.Series([10, 12, 12, 13, 12, 11, 10, 300])

# Calculate Z-Scores
mean = np.mean(data)
std_dev = np.std(data)
z_scores = (data - mean) / std_dev

# Detect anomalies
threshold = 3
anomalies = data[np.abs(z_scores) > threshold]
print("Anomalies detected:", anomalies.tolist())
```

2. Modified Z-Score Method

Modified Z-Score improves on the Z-Score method by using the median and median absolute deviation (MAD) instead of the mean and standard deviation, making it more robust to outliers.

Concept:

- The Modified Z-Score is calculated using the formula:

$$M_i = \frac{0.675x(X_i - median)}{MAD}$$

where M_i is the Modified Z-Score for data point X_i, and MAD is the median absolute deviation.

Anomaly Detection:

- A common threshold for the Modified Z-Score is 3.5.

Code Example (Python):

```python
from scipy.stats import median_abs_deviation


# Calculate Modified Z-Scores
median = np.median(data)
mad = median_abs_deviation(data, scale='normal')
modified_z_scores = 0.6745 * (data - median) / mad


# Detect anomalies
threshold = 3.5
anomalies = data[np.abs(modified_z_scores) > threshold]
print("Anomalies detected:", anomalies.tolist())
```

3. Box Plot Method

Box Plot uses quartiles to identify anomalies. Data points that fall outside the "whiskers" of the box plot, which extend 1.5 times the interquartile range (IQR) from the quartiles, are considered anomalies.

Concept:

- The IQR is calculated as:

$$IQR = Q3 - Q1$$

where Q1 and Q3 are the first and third quartiles.

Anomaly Detection:

- Anomalies are points that fall below $Q1 - 1.5 \times IQR$ or above $Q3 + 1.5 \times IQR$

Code Example (Python):

```python
import seaborn as sns


# Create box plot
sns.boxplot(data=data)
```

This visual method can help to quickly identify anomalies by showing the spread and the outliers in the dataset.

4. Statistical Process Control (SPC)

Statistical Process Control (SPC) involves monitoring and controlling a process through statistical methods to ensure it operates at its full potential. It often uses control charts to detect anomalies in a continuous process.

Concept:

- SPC control charts track process metrics and highlight anomalies when metrics fall outside control limits.

Code Example (Python):

```python
import matplotlib.pyplot as plt
```

```python
# Calculate control limits
mean = np.mean(data)
std_dev = np.std(data)
upper_limit = mean + 3 * std_dev
lower_limit = mean - 3 * std_dev

# Plot control chart
plt.figure(figsize=(10, 6))
plt.plot(data, marker='o', linestyle='-', color='blue')
plt.axhline(upper_limit, color='red', linestyle='--', label='Upper Control Limit')
plt.axhline(lower_limit, color='green', linestyle='--', label='Lower Control Limit')
plt.title('Control Chart')
plt.xlabel('Index')
plt.ylabel('Value')
plt.legend()
plt.show()
```

Statistical methods for anomaly detection leverage statistical properties to identify deviations from the norm. Methods like Z-Score, Modified Z-Score, Box Plot, and Statistical Process Control each offer unique approaches to detecting anomalies, making them suitable for various applications. The choice of method depends on the nature of the data and the specific requirements of the analysis.

Machine Learning-Based Anomaly Detection

Machine learning-based anomaly detection leverages algorithms to identify data points that significantly deviate from the expected patterns in a dataset. Unlike traditional statistical methods, machine learning approaches can model complex relationships and detect anomalies in high-dimensional and non-linear data. This section explores various machine learning techniques used for anomaly detection.

1. Isolation Forest

Isolation Forest is an algorithm specifically designed for anomaly detection. It isolates anomalies instead of profiling normal data points, making it effective for high-dimensional datasets.

Concept:

- The algorithm constructs an ensemble of random trees (Isolation Trees) to isolate data points.

- Anomalies are typically isolated faster and require fewer splits compared to normal points, leading to shorter path lengths in the trees.

Code Example (Python):

```python
from sklearn.ensemble import IsolationForest

import numpy as np

import pandas as pd


# Sample data
data = pd.DataFrame({

    'feature1': [1, 2, 1.5, 2.5, 3, 100],

    'feature2': [1, 1.5, 1, 2, 2.5, 200]

})


# Fit Isolation Forest model
```

```
model = IsolationForest(contamination=0.1)

data['anomaly'] = model.fit_predict(data)


# Detect anomalies

anomalies = data[data['anomaly'] == -1]

print("Anomalies detected:", anomalies)
```

2. One-Class SVM

One-Class SVM (Support Vector Machine) is a technique used for anomaly detection by learning a decision boundary around the majority class and identifying outliers as data points that fall outside this boundary.

Concept:

- The model learns a boundary around the normal data, and points that fall outside this boundary are considered anomalies.

- It is particularly useful when the normal data is well-defined but anomalies are rare or poorly understood.

Code Example (Python):

```
from sklearn.svm import OneClassSVM

import numpy as np

import pandas as pd


# Sample data

data = pd.DataFrame({

    'feature1': [1, 2, 1.5, 2.5, 3, 100],

    'feature2': [1, 1.5, 1, 2, 2.5, 200]

})
```

```
# Fit One-Class SVM model
model = OneClassSVM(gamma='auto', nu=0.1)
data['anomaly'] = model.fit_predict(data)

# Detect anomalies
anomalies = data[data['anomaly'] == -1]
print("Anomalies detected:", anomalies)
```

3. Autoencoders

Autoencoders are neural networks designed to learn efficient representations of data by compressing and reconstructing the input. Anomalies can be detected based on reconstruction errors.

Concept:

- Autoencoders are trained to reconstruct input data. During training, they learn to encode and decode the data with minimal loss.

- During inference, data points with high reconstruction errors are flagged as anomalies.

Code Example (Python):

```
import numpy as np
import pandas as pd
from sklearn.preprocessing import StandardScaler
from keras.models import Sequential
from keras.layers import Dense

# Sample data
```

```python
data = pd.DataFrame({
    'feature1': [1, 2, 1.5, 2.5, 3, 100],
    'feature2': [1, 1.5, 1, 2, 2.5, 200]
})

# Preprocess data
scaler = StandardScaler()
data_scaled = scaler.fit_transform(data)

# Define autoencoder model
autoencoder = Sequential([
    Dense(2, activation='relu', input_shape=(data_scaled.shape[1],)),
    Dense(1, activation='relu'),
    Dense(2, activation='relu')
])
autoencoder.compile(optimizer='adam', loss='mean_squared_error')

# Train autoencoder
autoencoder.fit(data_scaled, data_scaled, epochs=50, batch_size=1,
verbose=1)

# Predict reconstruction
reconstructions = autoencoder.predict(data_scaled)
reconstruction_errors = np.mean(np.abs(data_scaled - reconstructions),
axis=1)
```

```
# Detect anomalies
threshold = np.percentile(reconstruction_errors, 95)
anomalies = data[reconstruction_errors > threshold]
print("Anomalies detected:", anomalies)
```

4. k-Nearest Neighbors (k-NN)

k-Nearest Neighbors (k-NN) is a method used to identify anomalies based on the distance between a data point and its k-nearest neighbors. Points with larger distances from their neighbors are considered anomalies.

Concept:

- The algorithm calculates the distance of each data point to its k-nearest neighbors.

- Points that have significantly larger distances compared to their neighbors are flagged as anomalies.

Code Example (Python):

```
from sklearn.neighbors import LocalOutlierFactor
import numpy as np
import pandas as pd

# Sample data
data = pd.DataFrame({
    'feature1': [1, 2, 1.5, 2.5, 3, 100],
    'feature2': [1, 1.5, 1, 2, 2.5, 200]
})

# Fit k-NN model
```

```
model = LocalOutlierFactor(n_neighbors=2)

data['anomaly'] = model.fit_predict(data)


# Detect anomalies

anomalies = data[data['anomaly'] == -1]

print("Anomalies detected:", anomalies)
```

Machine learning-based anomaly detection methods provide advanced tools for identifying outliers in complex datasets. Techniques such as Isolation Forest, One-Class SVM, Autoencoders, and k-Nearest Neighbors each offer unique approaches for detecting anomalies, making them suitable for various applications. The choice of method depends on the characteristics of the data and the specific requirements of the analysis.

Application of Anomaly Detection in Various Domains

Anomaly detection techniques are applied across numerous domains to identify outliers, fraud, and unusual patterns that deviate from the norm. The ability to detect such anomalies is crucial for maintaining system integrity, enhancing security, and improving operational efficiency. Here's an overview of how anomaly detection is applied in different domains:

1. Finance

Applications:

- **Fraud Detection:** Anomaly detection is used to identify unusual financial transactions that may indicate fraudulent activity. For example, unusual spending patterns or transactions in an account that deviate significantly from the norm can trigger alerts.

- **Risk Management:** Identifying anomalies in financial metrics can help assess and manage risks, such as sudden changes in stock prices or deviations from expected investment returns.

Code Example (Python with Isolation Forest):

```
from sklearn.ensemble import IsolationForest
import numpy as np


# Sample data
X = np.array([[100, 200], [110, 210], [120, 220], [1000, 2000]])  # Normal
+ anomalous data


# Train Isolation Forest
model = IsolationForest(contamination=0.1)
model.fit(X)


# Predict anomalies
predictions = model.predict(X)
print(predictions)  # -1 indicates anomaly, 1 indicates normal
```

2. Healthcare

Applications:

- **Disease Outbreak Detection:** Anomaly detection can identify unusual patterns in patient data or health records that may indicate disease outbreaks or emerging health issues.

- **Medical Image Analysis:** Detecting anomalies in medical images, such as MRI or CT scans, helps in identifying irregularities that may require further investigation.

Code Example (Python with Autoencoder):

```
from keras.models import Model
from keras.layers import Input, Dense
import numpy as np
```

```
# Sample data
X_train = np.random.normal(size=(100, 20))  # Normal data
X_test = np.vstack([X_train, np.random.normal(size=(10, 20))])  # Normal
+ anomalous data


# Autoencoder model
input_layer = Input(shape=(20,))
encoded = Dense(14, activation='relu')(input_layer)
decoded = Dense(20, activation='sigmoid')(encoded)


autoencoder = Model(input_layer, decoded)
autoencoder.compile(optimizer='adam', loss='binary_crossentropy')
autoencoder.fit(X_train, X_train, epochs=50, batch_size=10, shuffle=True)


# Predict anomalies
reconstructed = autoencoder.predict(X_test)
mse = np.mean(np.power(X_test - reconstructed, 2), axis=1)
print(mse)  # Higher MSE indicates anomaly
```

3. Cybersecurity

Applications:

- **Intrusion Detection Systems (IDS):** Anomaly detection helps in identifying unusual network traffic or system behavior that may indicate a potential security breach or cyber attack.

- **Malware Detection:** Detecting deviations in file behavior or system processes that could signify the presence of malware or other malicious activities.

Code Example (Python with k-NN):

```python
from sklearn.neighbors import LocalOutlierFactor
import numpy as np

# Sample data
X = np.array([[1, 2], [2, 3], [3, 4], [10, 10]])  # Normal + anomalous data

# Train k-NN
model = LocalOutlierFactor(n_neighbors=2, contamination=0.1)
predictions = model.fit_predict(X)
print(predictions)  # -1 indicates anomaly, 1 indicates normal
```

4. Manufacturing

Applications:

- **Equipment Monitoring:** Anomaly detection can identify unusual patterns in sensor data from manufacturing equipment, helping to predict equipment failures and schedule maintenance.

- **Quality Control:** Detecting defects or anomalies in product quality data to ensure consistent production standards and identify issues in the production process.

Code Example (Python with One-Class SVM):

```python
from sklearn.svm import OneClassSVM
import numpy as np

# Sample data
```

```
X_train = np.random.normal(size=(100, 5))  # Normal data
X_test = np.vstack([X_train, np.random.normal(size=(10, 5))])  # Normal
+ anomalous data


# Train One-Class SVM
model = OneClassSVM(gamma='auto', nu=0.1)
model.fit(X_train)


# Predict anomalies
predictions = model.predict(X_test)
print(predictions)  # -1 indicates anomaly, 1 indicates normal
```

5. Retail

Applications:

- **Inventory Management:** Anomaly detection can help in identifying unusual patterns in inventory levels, such as sudden drops or spikes that might indicate issues with stock management or theft.

- **Customer Behavior Analysis:** Detecting deviations in customer purchasing patterns can reveal unusual buying behavior or preferences that may require targeted marketing strategies.

Code Example (Python with Isolation Forest):

```
from sklearn.ensemble import IsolationForest
import numpy as np


# Sample data
```

```
X = np.array([[50, 30], [60, 35], [70, 40], [500, 300]])  # Normal +
anomalous data


# Train Isolation Forest

model = IsolationForest(contamination=0.1)

model.fit(X)


# Predict anomalies

predictions = model.predict(X)

print(predictions)  # -1 indicates anomaly, 1 indicates normal
```

Anomaly detection techniques are versatile and can be applied across a wide range of domains, including finance, healthcare, cybersecurity, manufacturing, and retail. Each domain leverages these techniques to identify unusual patterns, detect fraud, monitor systems, and improve decision-making processes. The choice of method and its application depend on the specific requirements and characteristics of the data in each domain.

Appendix

Glossary

Machine Learning: A subfield of artificial intelligence (AI) that focuses on developing algorithms and models that enable computers to learn patterns and make predictions from data without being explicitly programmed.

Supervised Learning: A type of machine learning where the algorithm is trained on labeled data, consisting of input-output pairs. The goal is to learn a mapping from inputs to outputs, allowing the algorithm to make predictions on new, unseen data.

Unsupervised Learning: A type of machine learning where the algorithm is trained on unlabeled data. The algorithm must find patterns, structure, or relationships in the data without explicit guidance, often through techniques like clustering or dimensionality reduction.

Reinforcement Learning: A type of machine learning where an agent learns to interact with an environment in order to maximize cumulative rewards. The agent learns through trial and error, receiving feedback from the environment based on its actions.

Regression: A type of supervised learning task where the goal is to predict continuous numeric values. Regression algorithms aim to model the relationship between input features and output targets.

Classification: A type of supervised learning task where the goal is to predict discrete categorical labels or classes. Classification algorithms aim to learn decision boundaries that separate different classes in the input space.

Feature Engineering: The process of selecting, transforming, or creating new features from raw data to improve the performance of machine learning models. It involves domain knowledge, creativity, and experimentation to extract meaningful information from the data.

Overfitting: A common problem in machine learning where a model learns to memorize the training data instead of generalizing to unseen data. Overfitting occurs when a model is too complex relative to the amount of training data, leading to poor performance on new data.

Underfitting: A problem in machine learning where a model is too simple to capture the underlying patterns in the data. Underfitting occurs when a model is unable to learn from the training data, resulting in poor performance on both training and test data.

Bias-Variance Tradeoff: A fundamental concept in machine learning that describes the balance between bias (error due to overly simplistic assumptions) and variance (error due to sensitivity to small fluctuations in the training data). Finding the optimal balance is crucial for building models that generalize well to new data.

Data Sources

1. **UCI Machine Learning Repository**: The UCI Machine Learning Repository is a collection of databases, domain theories, and datasets used by the machine learning community for empirical analysis of machine learning algorithms. It hosts a wide variety of datasets across different domains, including classification, regression, clustering, and more. Visit the repository at UCI Machine Learning Repository for access to a diverse range of datasets.

2. **Kaggle Datasets**: Kaggle is a popular platform for data science competitions, and it also hosts a large collection of datasets contributed by the community. You can explore and download datasets on various topics, ranging from computer vision and natural language processing to finance and healthcare. Visit the Kaggle Datasets page at Kaggle Datasets to find datasets for your machine learning projects.

3. **GitHub**: GitHub is a platform for hosting and sharing code repositories, but it also hosts numerous datasets shared by researchers, organizations, and individuals. You can search for datasets using keywords related to your interests or specific machine learning tasks. Explore GitHub repositories tagged with "datasets" or visit curated lists of datasets such as Awesome Public Datasets for a wide range of options.

4. **Google Dataset Search**: Google Dataset Search is a search engine specifically designed to help users discover datasets hosted across

the web. You can use it to find datasets from various sources, including academic institutions, government organizations, and research projects. Visit Google Dataset Search and enter keywords related to your desired dataset to explore available options.

5. **OpenML**: OpenML is an online platform that enables researchers to share datasets and experiments, fostering collaboration and reproducibility in machine learning research. It offers a vast collection of datasets along with tools for sharing, analyzing, and reusing machine learning experiments. Visit OpenML to browse and download datasets for your machine learning projects.

These are just a few examples of sources where you can find datasets for practicing machine learning techniques. Remember to check the licensing and terms of use for each dataset before downloading and using it in your projects.

Further Reading

Chapter 1: Introduction to Machine Learning

- **Book**: "Pattern Recognition and Machine Learning" by Christopher M. Bishop

- **Book**: "Hands-On Machine Learning with Scikit-Learn, Keras, and TensorFlow" by Aurélien Géron

- **Online Resource**: Introduction to Machine Learning course on Coursera by Andrew Ng

Chapter 2: Python Basics

- **Book**: "Python Crash Course" by Eric Matthes

- **Online Resource**: Python Documentation (https://docs.python.org/3/)

Chapter 3: Libraries and Frameworks

- **Book**: "Python Data Science Handbook" by Jake VanderPlas

- **Online Resource**: Scikit-learn Documentation (https://scikit-learn.org/stable/documentation.html)

- **Online Resource**: TensorFlow Documentation (https://www.tensorflow.org/guide)

Chapter 4: Data Preprocessing

- **Book**: "Feature Engineering for Machine Learning" by Alice Zheng and Amanda Casari

- **Article**: "The Importance of Data Preprocessing in Machine Learning and How to Do It Right" by Aarshay Jain (https://www.analyticsvidhya.com/blog/2020/07/data-preprocessing-in-data-science-python-guide/)

Chapter 5: Exploratory Data Analysis (EDA)

- **Book**: "Python for Data Analysis" by Wes McKinney

- **Article**: "Exploratory Data Analysis – Python" by Shashwat Khandelwal (https://towardsdatascience.com/exploratory-data-analysis-python-2020-guide-8caa5c79b21a)

Chapter 6: Supervised Learning

- **Book**: "Applied Predictive Modeling" by Max Kuhn and Kjell Johnson

- **Research Paper**: "The Elements of Statistical Learning" by Trevor Hastie, Robert Tibshirani, and Jerome Friedman

Chapter 7: Unsupervised Learning

- **Book**: "Hands-On Unsupervised Learning using Python" by Ankur A. Patel

- **Research Paper**: "Clustering and Its Applications in Bioinformatics" by Gan, G., Ma, C., and Wu, J.

Chapter 8: Ensemble Learning

- **Book**: "Ensemble Methods in Machine Learning" by Thomas G. Dietterich

- **Online Resource**: XGBoost Documentation (https://xgboost.readthedocs.io/en/latest/)

Chapter 9: Neural Networks and Deep Learning

- **Book**: "Deep Learning" by Ian Goodfellow, Yoshua Bengio, and Aaron Courville
- **Online Resource**: PyTorch Documentation (https://pytorch.org/docs/stable/index.html)

Chapter 10: Natural Language Processing (NLP)

- **Book**: "Natural Language Processing with Python" by Steven Bird, Ewan Klein, and Edward Loper
- **Article**: "A Gentle Introduction to Natural Language Processing" by Jason Brownlee (https://machinelearningmastery.com/gentle-introduction-natural-language-processing/)

Chapter 11: Model Deployment

- **Book**: "Flask Web Development" by Miguel Grinberg
- **Online Resource**: Heroku Documentation (https://devcenter.heroku.com/categories/deployment)

Chapter 12: Reinforcement Learning

- **Book**: "Reinforcement Learning: An Introduction" by Richard S. Sutton and Andrew G. Barto
- **Online Resource**: OpenAI Gym Documentation (https://gym.openai.com/docs/)

Chapter 13: Model Interpretability

- **Book**: "Interpretable Machine Learning" by Christoph Molnar
- **Article**: "Interpretable Machine Learning: A Guide for Making Black Box Models Explainable" by Saurabh Agarwal (https://towardsdatascience.com/interpretable-machine-learning-a-guide-for-making-black-box-models-explainable-5b1a571d5d30)

Chapter 14: Advanced Topics

- **Book**: "Automated Machine Learning: Methods, Systems, Challenges" by Frank Hutter, Lars Kotthoff, and Joaquin Vanschoren

- **Online Resource**: Google Cloud AutoML Documentation (https://cloud.google.com/automl/docs)

Chapter 15: Case Studies

- **Book**: "Python Machine Learning Case Studies" by Danish Haroon and Ahmad Ghafoor

- **Research Paper**: Any recent research papers related to specific case studies of interest in machine learning

Useful Tools and Libraries

Data Analysis and Preprocessing

- **NumPy**: A powerful library for numerical computing in Python, providing support for multidimensional arrays and matrices.

    - Website: NumPy

    - Installation: **pip install numpy**

- **Pandas**: A data manipulation and analysis library, offering data structures like DataFrame and Series for efficient data handling.

    - Website: Pandas

    - Installation: **pip install pandas**

Machine Learning

- **Scikit-learn**: A comprehensive library for machine learning in Python, offering various algorithms and tools for classification, regression, clustering, and more.

    - Website: Scikit-learn

    - Installation: **pip install scikit-learn**

- **TensorFlow**: An open-source deep learning framework developed by Google, widely used for building and training neural networks.

    - Website: TensorFlow

    - Installation: **pip install tensorflow**

- **PyTorch**: Another popular deep learning framework, known for its dynamic computation graph and ease of use.

  - Website: PyTorch

  - Installation: **pip install torch**

Data Visualization

- **Matplotlib**: A flexible plotting library for creating static, interactive, and animated visualizations in Python.

  - Website: Matplotlib

  - Installation: **pip install matplotlib**

- **Seaborn**: Built on top of Matplotlib, Seaborn provides a high-level interface for creating attractive statistical graphics.

  - Website: Seaborn

  - Installation: **pip install seaborn**

Model Deployment

- **Flask**: A lightweight web framework for building RESTful APIs and web applications in Python.

  - Website: Flask

  - Installation: **pip install Flask**

- **Django**: A high-level web framework for rapid development and clean design, suitable for building complex web applications.

  - Website: Django

  - Installation: **pip install Django**

Online Platforms

- **Google Colab**: A free Jupyter notebook environment provided by Google, offering GPU and TPU support for running machine learning experiments in the cloud.

  - Website: Google Colab

- **Kaggle**: A popular platform for data science competitions, datasets, and notebooks, providing access to powerful computing resources and a community of data enthusiasts.

  - Website: Kaggle

Frequently Asked Questions (FAQs)

1. What is machine learning, and how does it differ from traditional programming?

Answer: Machine learning is a subset of artificial intelligence (AI) that focuses on enabling systems to learn from data and make predictions or decisions without being explicitly programmed. In traditional programming, developers write explicit rules and instructions for the computer to follow. In contrast, machine learning algorithms learn patterns and relationships from data, allowing them to make decisions or predictions based on new inputs.

2. What are the different types of machine learning algorithms?

Answer: Machine learning algorithms are broadly categorized into three main types:

- **Supervised Learning:** In supervised learning, the algorithm learns from labeled data, where each example is associated with a target label or outcome. Common tasks include classification (predicting categories) and regression (predicting numerical values).

- **Unsupervised Learning:** Unsupervised learning involves learning from unlabeled data, where the algorithm seeks to uncover hidden patterns or structures in the data. Clustering and dimensionality reduction are common tasks in unsupervised learning.

- **Reinforcement Learning:** Reinforcement learning is a type of learning where an agent learns to interact with an environment by taking actions and receiving feedback in the form of rewards or penalties. The goal is to learn a policy that maximizes cumulative rewards over time.

3. What is the difference between overfitting and underfitting?

Answer: Overfitting and underfitting are two common problems in machine learning models:

- **Overfitting:** Occurs when a model learns the training data too well, capturing noise or random fluctuations in the data rather than underlying patterns. This can result in poor generalization to new, unseen data.

- **Underfitting:** Occurs when a model is too simple to capture the underlying structure of the data, leading to high bias and poor performance on both training and test data.

To address overfitting, techniques such as regularization, cross-validation, and early stopping can be employed. Underfitting can be mitigated by using more complex models or adding additional features to the dataset.

4. How do I evaluate the performance of a machine learning model?

Answer: The performance of a machine learning model can be evaluated using various metrics depending on the task:

- **Regression:** Common evaluation metrics include Mean Absolute Error (MAE), Mean Squared Error (MSE), and R-squared (coefficient of determination).

- **Classification:** Metrics such as accuracy, precision, recall, F1 score, and area under the ROC curve (AUC-ROC) are commonly used to evaluate classification models.

- **Clustering:** Evaluation metrics for clustering algorithms include silhouette score, Davies-Bouldin index, and adjusted Rand index.

It's essential to select evaluation metrics that are appropriate for the specific task and consider the trade-offs between different metrics.

Mathematical Background

Linear Algebra

Linear algebra plays a crucial role in machine learning, particularly in understanding and implementing algorithms for data manipulation and model training. Here are some key concepts:

- **Vectors and Matrices:** Vectors are arrays of numbers, and matrices are rectangular arrays of numbers arranged in rows and columns. They are fundamental data structures used to represent data and parameters in machine learning.

- **Matrix Operations:** Common matrix operations include addition, subtraction, multiplication, and transposition. These operations are used in various algorithms for computations such as matrix multiplication, matrix inversion, and solving systems of linear equations.

- **Vector Dot Product:** The dot product of two vectors measures the similarity or alignment between them. It is calculated by multiplying corresponding elements of the vectors and summing the results.

- **Matrix Multiplication:** Matrix multiplication is a fundamental operation in linear algebra, often used in transformations, regressions, and neural network computations. It involves multiplying rows of the first matrix by columns of the second matrix and summing the results.

Calculus

Calculus provides the mathematical framework for understanding optimization algorithms used in training machine learning models. Key concepts include:

- **Derivatives:** Derivatives represent the rate of change of a function with respect to its input variables. They are used to find the minimum or maximum points of a function, which are essential for optimizing machine learning models.

- **Gradient Descent:** Gradient descent is an iterative optimization algorithm used to minimize the loss function of a machine learning model. It works by updating the model parameters in the direction of the negative gradient of the loss function.

- **Partial Derivatives:** Partial derivatives extend the concept of derivatives to functions of multiple variables. They are used to compute the gradient of a multivariable function, which is crucial for gradient-based optimization algorithms.

Probability Theory and Statistics

Probability theory and statistics provide the foundation for understanding uncertainty and making probabilistic predictions in machine learning. Key concepts include:

- **Probability Distributions:** Probability distributions describe the likelihood of different outcomes in a random experiment. Common distributions used in machine learning include Gaussian (normal), Bernoulli, and multinomial distributions.

- **Expectation and Variance:** Expectation (mean) and variance are statistical measures that describe the central tendency and spread of a distribution, respectively. They are used to summarize data and assess model performance.

- **Bayesian Inference:** Bayesian inference is a statistical framework for updating beliefs about uncertain parameters or hypotheses based on observed data. It is used in Bayesian machine learning algorithms to make probabilistic predictions and estimate model parameters.

Additional Resources

For readers interested in further exploring mathematical concepts relevant to machine learning, the following resources are recommended:

- "Linear Algebra and Its Applications" by Gilbert Strang

- "Calculus: Early Transcendentals" by James Stewart

- "Introduction to Probability" by Joseph K. Blitzstein and Jessica Hwang

- "Pattern Recognition and Machine Learning" by Christopher M. Bishop

Model Evaluation Metrics

Introduction

Model evaluation metrics are used to assess the performance of machine learning models. Understanding these metrics is essential for interpreting the effectiveness of a model and making informed decisions about its deployment. In this appendix, we will discuss some of the commonly used evaluation metrics and provide guidelines for their interpretation.

Accuracy

Accuracy measures the proportion of correctly classified instances out of the total number of instances. It is calculated as:

$$Accuracy = \frac{TP + TN}{TP + TN + FP + FN}$$

Where:

- TP (True Positives) is the number of correctly predicted positive instances.
- TN (True Negatives) is the number of correctly predicted negative instances.
- FP (False Positives) is the number of incorrectly predicted positive instances.
- FN (False Negatives) is the number of incorrectly predicted negative instances.

Precision

Precision measures the proportion of true positive predictions out of all positive predictions. It is calculated as:

$$Precision = \frac{TP}{TP + FP}$$

Precision is particularly useful when the cost of false positives is high.

Recall (Sensitivity)

Recall, also known as sensitivity or true positive rate, measures the proportion of actual positive instances that are correctly identified by the model. It is calculated as:

$$Recall = \frac{TP}{TP + FN}$$

Recall is important in scenarios where the detection of positive instances is critical.

F1 Score

The F1 score is the harmonic mean of precision and recall. It provides a balance between precision and recall and is calculated as:

$$F1_{Score} = \frac{2x(PrecisionxRecall)}{Precision + Recall}$$

The F1 score is useful when there is an uneven class distribution or when false positives and false negatives have different costs.

ROC Curve

The Receiver Operating Characteristic (ROC) curve is a graphical representation of the true positive rate (TPR) versus the false positive rate (FPR) at various threshold settings. It helps visualize the trade-off between sensitivity and specificity.

Confusion Matrix

A confusion matrix is a table that summarizes the performance of a classification model. It displays the counts of true positive, true negative, false positive, and false negative predictions.

	Predicted Negative	Predicted Positive
Actual Negative	True Negative (TN)	False Positive (FP)
Actual Positive	False Negative (FN)	True Positive (TP)

Conclusion

Understanding model evaluation metrics is crucial for assessing the performance of machine learning models and making informed decisions. By considering a combination of metrics such as accuracy, precision, recall, F1 score, ROC curve, and confusion matrix, you can gain insights into the strengths and weaknesses of your models and improve their effectiveness.

Sample Solutions to End of Chapter Problems

Chapter 4

```python
import pandas as pd
import numpy as np

# Sample DataFrame with missing values
data = {'A': [1, 2, np.nan, 4, 5],
    'B': [np.nan, 10, 20, 30, np.nan],
    'C': ['a', 'b', 'c', np.nan, 'e']}
df = pd.DataFrame(data)

# Data Cleaning: Handling Missing Values
# Drop rows with missing values
cleaned_data = df.dropna()

# Fill missing values with mean
mean_filled_data = df.fillna(df.mean())

# Fill missing values with median
median_filled_data = df.fillna(df.median())

# Fill missing values with mode
mode_filled_data = df.apply(lambda x: x.fillna(x.mode()[0]))
```

```python
# Handling Categorical Data
# Convert categorical variable into dummy/indicator variables
dummy_data = pd.get_dummies(df['C'])


# Data Transformation Techniques
# Log transformation
log_transformed_data = df.apply(lambda x: np.log(x) if
np.issubdtype(x.dtype, np.number) else x)


# Min-Max Scaling
min_max_scaled_data = df.apply(lambda x: (x - x.min()) / (x.max() -
x.min()) if np.issubdtype(x.dtype, np.number) else x)


# Standardization (Z-score normalization)
standardized_data = df.apply(lambda x: (x - x.mean()) / x.std() if
np.issubdtype(x.dtype, np.number) else x)
```

Chapter 5

```python
import pandas as pd

import numpy as np

import matplotlib.pyplot as plt

import seaborn as sns


# Sample DataFrame
```

```python
data = {'A': [1, 2, 3, 4, 5],
    'B': [10, 20, 30, 40, 50],
    'C': ['a', 'b', 'c', 'd', 'e']}
df = pd.DataFrame(data)

# Descriptive Statistics
# Calculate mean, median, mode, and standard deviation
mean = df.mean()
median = df.median()
mode = df.mode().iloc[0]
std_dev = df.std()


# Data Visualization with Matplotlib
# Histogram
plt.hist(df['A'])
plt.xlabel('A')
plt.ylabel('Frequency')
plt.title('Histogram of A')
plt.show()


# Scatter Plot
plt.scatter(df['A'], df['B'])
plt.xlabel('A')
plt.ylabel('B')
plt.title('Scatter Plot between A and B')
```

```python
plt.show()


# Data Visualization with Seaborn
# Boxplot
sns.boxplot(x='C', y='B', data=df)
plt.xlabel('Categorical Variable')
plt.ylabel('B')
plt.title('Boxplot of B by Categorical Variable')
plt.show()


# Correlation Analysis
# Compute correlation matrix
correlation_matrix = df.corr()


# Plot correlation matrix as heatmap
sns.heatmap(correlation_matrix, annot=True, cmap='coolwarm',
linewidths=0.5)
plt.title('Correlation Matrix')
plt.show()


# Feature Importance Analysis
# Suppose we have a pre-trained model 'model'
feature_importance = model.feature_importances_
sorted_indices = np.argsort(feature_importance)[::-1]
sorted_features = df.columns[sorted_indices]
```

```python
# Print feature importance
for i, feature in enumerate(sorted_features):
    print(f"{i+1}. {feature}: {feature_importance[sorted_indices[i]]:.4f}")
```

Chapter 6

```python
from sklearn.model_selection import train_test_split
from sklearn.linear_model import LinearRegression, LogisticRegression
from sklearn.metrics import mean_squared_error, accuracy_score


# Sample data
X = [[1], [2], [3], [4], [5]]
y = [2, 4, 6, 8, 10]


# Regression
# Splitting the data into training and testing sets
X_train, X_test, y_train, y_test = train_test_split(X, y, test_size=0.2,
random_state=42)


# Linear Regression
reg_model = LinearRegression()
reg_model.fit(X_train, y_train)
reg_pred = reg_model.predict(X_test)


# Classification
```

```python
# Sample data
X_cls = [[1], [2], [3], [4], [5]]
y_cls = [0, 0, 1, 1, 1]


# Splitting the data into training and testing sets
X_train_cls, X_test_cls, y_train_cls, y_test_cls = train_test_split(X_cls,
y_cls, test_size=0.2, random_state=42)


# Logistic Regression
cls_model = LogisticRegression()
cls_model.fit(X_train_cls, y_train_cls)
cls_pred = cls_model.predict(X_test_cls)


# Model Evaluation
# Regression
reg_rmse = mean_squared_error(y_test, reg_pred, squared=False)


# Classification
cls_accuracy = accuracy_score(y_test_cls, cls_pred)


print(f"Regression RMSE: {reg_rmse:.2f}")
print(f"Classification Accuracy: {cls_accuracy:.2f}")
```

Chapter 7

```python
from sklearn.cluster import KMeans
```

```python
from sklearn.datasets import make_blobs
from sklearn.metrics import silhouette_score
from sklearn.preprocessing import StandardScaler
import matplotlib.pyplot as plt


# Generate sample data for clustering
X, _ = make_blobs(n_samples=300, centers=4, cluster_std=0.60,
random_state=0)


# Clustering using K-means
kmeans = KMeans(n_clusters=4)
kmeans.fit(X)
y_kmeans = kmeans.predict(X)


# Plotting clustered data
plt.scatter(X[:, 0], X[:, 1], c=y_kmeans, cmap='viridis')
plt.scatter(kmeans.cluster_centers_[:, 0], kmeans.cluster_centers_[:, 1],
s=200, c='red', alpha=0.75)
plt.xlabel('Feature 1')
plt.ylabel('Feature 2')
plt.title('K-means Clustering')
plt.show()


# Hierarchical Clustering
from scipy.cluster.hierarchy import dendrogram, linkage
```

```python
# Perform hierarchical clustering
Z = linkage(X, method='ward')


# Plot dendrogram
plt.figure(figsize=(10, 5))
plt.title('Hierarchical Clustering Dendrogram')
plt.xlabel('Sample Index')
plt.ylabel('Distance')
dendrogram(Z)
plt.show()


# DBSCAN Clustering
from sklearn.cluster import DBSCAN


# Clustering using DBSCAN
dbscan = DBSCAN(eps=0.3, min_samples=10)
y_dbscan = dbscan.fit_predict(X)


# Plotting clustered data
plt.scatter(X[:, 0], X[:, 1], c=y_dbscan, cmap='viridis')
plt.xlabel('Feature 1')
plt.ylabel('Feature 2')
plt.title('DBSCAN Clustering')
plt.show()
```

```python
# Dimensionality Reduction using PCA
from sklearn.decomposition import PCA


# Standardize the data
scaler = StandardScaler()
X_scaled = scaler.fit_transform(X)


# Apply PCA
pca = PCA(n_components=2)
X_pca = pca.fit_transform(X_scaled)


# Plotting the reduced data
plt.scatter(X_pca[:, 0], X_pca[:, 1], c=y_kmeans, cmap='viridis')
plt.xlabel('Principal Component 1')
plt.ylabel('Principal Component 2')
plt.title('PCA Visualization')
plt.show()
```

Chapter 8

```python
from sklearn.ensemble import RandomForestClassifier,
GradientBoostingClassifier
from sklearn.datasets import load_iris
from sklearn.model_selection import train_test_split
from sklearn.metrics import accuracy_score, confusion_matrix
import matplotlib.pyplot as plt
```

```python
import seaborn as sns


# Load the Iris dataset
iris = load_iris()
X = iris.data
y = iris.target


# Splitting the dataset into training and testing sets
X_train, X_test, y_train, y_test = train_test_split(X, y, test_size=0.2,
random_state=42)


# Random Forest
rf_clf = RandomForestClassifier(n_estimators=100, random_state=42)
rf_clf.fit(X_train, y_train)
rf_pred = rf_clf.predict(X_test)


# Gradient Boosting
gb_clf = GradientBoostingClassifier(n_estimators=100, random_state=42)
gb_clf.fit(X_train, y_train)
gb_pred = gb_clf.predict(X_test)


# Model Evaluation
# Random Forest
rf_accuracy = accuracy_score(y_test, rf_pred)
rf_conf_matrix = confusion_matrix(y_test, rf_pred)
```

```
# Gradient Boosting
gb_accuracy = accuracy_score(y_test, gb_pred)
gb_conf_matrix = confusion_matrix(y_test, gb_pred)


# Plot Confusion Matrices
fig, axes = plt.subplots(1, 2, figsize=(12, 5))
sns.heatmap(rf_conf_matrix, annot=True, cmap='Blues', fmt='d',
ax=axes[0])
axes[0].set_title('Random Forest Confusion Matrix')
axes[0].set_xlabel('Predicted Labels')
axes[0].set_ylabel('True Labels')


sns.heatmap(gb_conf_matrix, annot=True, cmap='Blues', fmt='d',
ax=axes[1])
axes[1].set_title('Gradient Boosting Confusion Matrix')
axes[1].set_xlabel('Predicted Labels')
axes[1].set_ylabel('True Labels')


plt.tight_layout()
plt.show()


print("Random Forest Accuracy:", rf_accuracy)
print("Gradient Boosting Accuracy:", gb_accuracy)
```

Chapter 9

```
import tensorflow as tf

from tensorflow.keras.models import Sequential

from tensorflow.keras.layers import Dense


# Example dataset

X_train = [[0], [1], [2], [3], [4], [5], [6], [7], [8], [9]]

y_train = [[0], [2], [4], [6], [8], [10], [12], [14], [16], [18]]


# Build a simple neural network

model = Sequential([

    Dense(units=1, input_shape=[1])

])


# Compile the model

model.compile(optimizer='sgd', loss='mean_squared_error')


# Train the model

model.fit(X_train, y_train, epochs=1000, verbose=0)


# Predict using the trained model

X_test = [[10], [11], [12]]

predictions = model.predict(X_test)

print("Predictions:", predictions.flatten())
```

Chapter 10

```python
import nltk

from nltk.sentiment import SentimentIntensityAnalyzer

from nltk.tokenize import word_tokenize

from nltk.corpus import stopwords

from sklearn.datasets import fetch_20newsgroups

from sklearn.feature_extraction.text import TfidfVectorizer

from sklearn.model_selection import train_test_split

from sklearn.naive_bayes import MultinomialNB

from sklearn.metrics import accuracy_score, classification_report

from transformers import BertTokenizer,
TFBertForSequenceClassification

import tensorflow as tf


# Sample data for sentiment analysis

reviews = [

    "The movie was absolutely fantastic! I loved every moment of it.",

    "The acting was terrible, and the plot was boring. I wouldn't recommend
this movie to anyone.",

    "The book is a masterpiece. It brought tears to my eyes.",

    "The restaurant had great ambiance, but the food was disappointing."

]


# Sentiment Analysis with NLTK's SentimentIntensityAnalyzer
```

```python
sia = SentimentIntensityAnalyzer()
for review in reviews:
    sentiment_score = sia.polarity_scores(review)
    if sentiment_score['compound'] > 0.5:
        sentiment = "Positive"
    elif sentiment_score['compound'] < -0.5:
        sentiment = "Negative"
    else:
        sentiment = "Neutral"
    print(f"Review: {review}")
    print(f"Sentiment: {sentiment}\n")


# Sample data for text classification
categories = ['sci.space', 'comp.graphics']
data = fetch_20newsgroups(subset='all', categories=categories)
X_train, X_test, y_train, y_test = train_test_split(data.data, data.target,
test_size=0.2, random_state=42)


# Text Classification with Naive Bayes
vectorizer = TfidfVectorizer()
X_train_vect = vectorizer.fit_transform(X_train)
X_test_vect = vectorizer.transform(X_test)

classifier = MultinomialNB()
classifier.fit(X_train_vect, y_train)
```

```python
y_pred = classifier.predict(X_test_vect)

print("Naive Bayes Classification Report:")

print(classification_report(y_test, y_pred,
target_names=data.target_names))

print(f"Accuracy: {accuracy_score(y_test, y_pred)}\n")


# Text Classification with BERT

tokenizer = BertTokenizer.from_pretrained('bert-base-uncased')

model = TFBertForSequenceClassification.from_pretrained('bert-base-
uncased')


inputs = tokenizer(X_train, padding=True, truncation=True,
max_length=128, return_tensors='tf')

outputs = model(inputs)


print("BERT Classification Report:")

print(classification_report(y_test, outputs,
target_names=data.target_names))
```

Chapter 11

```python
# Problem 1: API Implementation

from flask import Flask, request, jsonify

import joblib


app = Flask(__name__)
```

```python
# Load the pre-trained sentiment analysis model
model = joblib.load('sentiment_analysis_model.pkl')

@app.route('/predict_sentiment', methods=['POST'])
def predict_sentiment():
    data = request.get_json()
    text = data['text']
    sentiment = model.predict([text])[0]
    return jsonify({'sentiment': sentiment})

if __name__ == '__main__':
    app.run(debug=True)



# Problem 2: Containerization
# Dockerfile
"""
FROM python:3.8-slim


COPY . /app
WORKDIR /app


RUN pip install -r requirements.txt
```

```python
EXPOSE 5000
CMD ["python", "app.py"]
"""


# Build Docker image: docker build -t sentiment-api .
# Run Docker container: docker run -p 5000:5000 sentiment-api


# Problem 3: Serverless Deployment (AWS Lambda)
# Handler function
import json

def lambda_handler(event, context):
    text = event['text']
    sentiment = model.predict([text])[0]
    return {
        'statusCode': 200,
        'body': json.dumps({'sentiment': sentiment})
    }


# Problem 4: Scaling Considerations
# Scaling strategies should be discussed and documented based on the
deployment environment and requirements.
```

Problem 5: Monitoring and Logging

Set up monitoring and logging using libraries like Prometheus, Grafana, or AWS CloudWatch.

Problem 6: Security and Authentication

Implement authentication and authorization mechanisms using API keys, OAuth tokens, or JWT.

Problem 7: Model Versioning

Develop a system for managing model versions using version control systems like Git and tagging releases.

Problem 8: Continuous Integration/Continuous Deployment (CI/CD)

Configure a CI/CD pipeline using Jenkins, GitLab CI, or GitHub Actions to automate model deployment.

Problem 9: Cost Optimization

Analyze cost implications and optimize resource usage using auto-scaling, spot instances, and resource optimization techniques.

Problem 10: Regulatory Compliance

Chapter 12

```python
import gym

import numpy as np


# Problem 1: Q-learning Practice Problem


# Create the GridWorld environment

env_gridworld = gym.make('GridWorld-v0')


# Initialize Q-table with zeros

Q_gridworld = np.zeros([env_gridworld.observation_space.n,
env_gridworld.action_space.n])


# Set hyperparameters

learning_rate_gridworld = 0.8

discount_factor_gridworld = 0.95

num_episodes_gridworld = 1000


# Q-learning algorithm for GridWorld environment

for episode in range(num_episodes_gridworld):

    state = env_gridworld.reset()

    done = False
```

```python
    while not done:
        action = np.argmax(Q_gridworld[state, :])  # Greedy policy
        new_state, reward, done, _ = env_gridworld.step(action)

        # Update Q-value using Bellman equation
        Q_gridworld[state, action] += learning_rate_gridworld * \
                        (reward + discount_factor_gridworld *
np.max(Q_gridworld[new_state, :]) - Q_gridworld[state, action])

        state = new_state


# Problem 2: Policy Iteration Practice Problem
# To be implemented by the learner.


# Problem 3: Model-Free Control Practice Problem
# To be implemented by the learner.


# Problem 4: Deep Q-Learning Practice Problem
# To be implemented by the learner.


# Problem 5: Multi-Agent Reinforcement Learning Practice Problem
# To be implemented by the learner.


# Problem 6: Continuous Action Space Practice Problem
```

```
# To be implemented by the learner.


# Problem 7: Hierarchical Reinforcement Learning Practice Problem

# To be implemented by the learner.


# Problem 8: Real-World Application Practice Problem

# To be implemented by the learner.
```

Chapter 13

```
import numpy as np

import pandas as pd

from sklearn.model_selection import train_test_split

from sklearn.ensemble import RandomForestClassifier

import shap

import lime

import lime.lime_tabular


# Load dataset

data = pd.read_csv('dataset.csv')


# Split data into features and target

X = data.drop('target', axis=1)

y = data['target']
```

```python
# Split data into training and testing sets
X_train, X_test, y_train, y_test = train_test_split(X, y, test_size=0.2,
random_state=42)


# Train a Random Forest classifier
model = RandomForestClassifier(n_estimators=100, random_state=42)
model.fit(X_train, y_train)


# 1. Understanding Model Predictions
# Analyze predictions on test set
predictions = model.predict(X_test)
confidence = model.predict_proba(X_test).max(axis=1)
uncertain_instances = X_test[confidence < 0.7]


# 2. Feature Importance Analysis
# Calculate feature importance
feature_importance = model.feature_importances_
important_features = X.columns[np.argsort(feature_importance)[::-1]][:5]


# 3. Model Explanation Techniques: SHAP
explainer = shap.Explainer(model, X_train)
shap_values = explainer(X_test)
shap.summary_plot(shap_values, X_test)


# 4. Model Explanation Techniques: LIME
```

```python
explainer = lime.lime_tabular.LimeTabularExplainer(X_train.values,
feature_names=X_train.columns)

exp = explainer.explain_instance(X_test.iloc[0], model.predict_proba,
num_features=5)

exp.show_in_notebook()


# 5. Permutation Importance Analysis
from sklearn.inspection import permutation_importance

perm_importance = permutation_importance(model, X_test, y_test)
perm_sorted_idx = perm_importance.importances_mean.argsort()[::-1]
perm_important_features = X.columns[perm_sorted_idx][:5]


# 6. Model Complexity Analysis
train_scores = []
test_scores = []
complexity_range = [1, 5, 10, 20, 50, 100]

for depth in complexity_range:
    clf = RandomForestClassifier(n_estimators=100, max_depth=depth,
random_state=42)
    clf.fit(X_train, y_train)
    train_scores.append(clf.score(X_train, y_train))
    test_scores.append(clf.score(X_test, y_test))


# Visualize model complexity vs. performance
```

```
import matplotlib.pyplot as plt


plt.plot(complexity_range, train_scores, label="Train Score")

plt.plot(complexity_range, test_scores, label="Test Score")

plt.xlabel("Max Depth")

plt.ylabel("Accuracy")

plt.title("Model Complexity Analysis")

plt.legend()

plt.show()
```

Chapter 14

```
# Problem 1: Grid Search Practice


from sklearn.datasets import load_digits

from sklearn.model_selection import train_test_split, GridSearchCV

from sklearn.tree import DecisionTreeClassifier


# Load the dataset

digits = load_digits()

X, y = digits.data, digits.target


# Split the dataset into training and testing sets

X_train, X_test, y_train, y_test = train_test_split(X, y, test_size=0.2,
random_state=42)
```

```python
# Define the hyperparameters grid
param_grid = {
    'max_depth': [None, 10, 20, 30],
    'min_samples_split': [2, 5, 10],
    'min_samples_leaf': [1, 2, 4]
}

# Create the decision tree classifier
dt_classifier = DecisionTreeClassifier()

# Perform grid search with cross-validation
grid_search = GridSearchCV(estimator=dt_classifier,
param_grid=param_grid, cv=5, scoring='accuracy')
grid_search.fit(X_train, y_train)

# Print the best hyperparameters
print("Best hyperparameters:", grid_search.best_params_)

# Evaluate the best model on the test set
best_model = grid_search.best_estimator_
test_accuracy = best_model.score(X_test, y_test)
print("Test set accuracy:", test_accuracy)
```

Chapter 15

```python
import pandas as pd

from sklearn.model_selection import train_test_split

from sklearn.ensemble import RandomForestClassifier

from sklearn.metrics import accuracy_score, classification_report

from imblearn.over_sampling import SMOTE


# Problem 1: Feature Engineering

# Additional feature: Proximity to amenities

housing_data['proximity_to_amenities'] = ...


# Problem 2: Model Comparison

X = housing_data.drop(columns=['price'])

y = housing_data['price']

X_train, X_test, y_train, y_test = train_test_split(X, y, test_size=0.2,
random_state=42)


# Linear Regression

from sklearn.linear_model import LinearRegression

linear_model = LinearRegression()

linear_model.fit(X_train, y_train)

linear_pred = linear_model.predict(X_test)

linear_mse = mean_squared_error(y_test, linear_pred)


# Decision Tree Regression

from sklearn.tree import DecisionTreeRegressor
```

```python
dt_model = DecisionTreeRegressor()
dt_model.fit(X_train, y_train)
dt_pred = dt_model.predict(X_test)
dt_mse = mean_squared_error(y_test, dt_pred)

# Random Forest Regression
from sklearn.ensemble import RandomForestRegressor
rf_model = RandomForestRegressor()
rf_model.fit(X_train, y_train)
rf_pred = rf_model.predict(X_test)
rf_mse = mean_squared_error(y_test, rf_pred)

print("Linear Regression MSE:", linear_mse)
print("Decision Tree Regression MSE:", dt_mse)
print("Random Forest Regression MSE:", rf_mse)

# Problem 3: Advanced Visualization
import folium
from folium.plugins import HeatMap

map = folium.Map(location=[latitude, longitude], zoom_start=10)
heat_data = [[row['latitude'], row['longitude']] for index, row in
housing_data.iterrows()]
HeatMap(heat_data).add_to(map)
map.save("housing_heatmap.html")
```

```python
# Problem 4: Feature Importance

important_features = rf_model.feature_importances_

feature_importance_df = pd.DataFrame({'Feature': X.columns,
'Importance': important_features})

feature_importance_df =
feature_importance_df.sort_values(by='Importance', ascending=False)


# Problem 5: Imbalanced Data Handling

smote = SMOTE()

X_resampled, y_resampled = smote.fit_resample(X_train, y_train)

rf_model.fit(X_resampled, y_resampled)

y_pred_resampled = rf_model.predict(X_test)

print("Accuracy after SMOTE:", accuracy_score(y_test,
y_pred_resampled))


# Problem 6: Cost-Benefit Analysis

# Calculate the potential financial impact of reducing churn based on
model predictions

# Determine the cost of customer acquisition, the revenue from retained
customers, and the estimated churn reduction
```

Chapter 18

Below are sample solutions for the reinforcement learning exercises using
the OpenAI Gym:

Exercise 1: CartPole Environment

```python
import gym

# Create CartPole environment
env = gym.make('CartPole-v1')

# Initialize Q-table
Q = {}

# Hyperparameters
alpha = 0.1
gamma = 0.99
epsilon = 0.1

# Training the agent
for episode in range(1000):
    state = env.reset()
    state = tuple(state)

    if state not in Q:
        Q[state] = [0, 0]  # Initialize Q-values for the state

    done = False

    while not done:
        # Epsilon-greedy policy
```

```python
    if np.random.rand() < epsilon:
        action = env.action_space.sample()  # Explore
    else:
        action = np.argmax(Q[state])  # Exploit

    next_state, reward, done, _ = env.step(action)
    next_state = tuple(next_state)

    if next_state not in Q:
        Q[next_state] = [0, 0]  # Initialize Q-values for the next state

    # Update Q-value using the Q-learning update rule
    Q[state][action] += alpha * (reward + gamma * max(Q[next_state]) -
Q[state][action])

    state = next_state

# Evaluate the trained agent
total_reward = 0
state = env.reset()
done = False

while not done:
    env.render()
    action = np.argmax(Q[tuple(state)])
```

```
    state, reward, done, _ = env.step(action)

    total_reward += reward


print("Total Reward:", total_reward)


env.close()
```

Exercise 2: Mountain Car Problem

```
import gym
import numpy as np


# Create MountainCar environment
env = gym.make('MountainCar-v0')


# Initialize Q-table
Q = {}


# Hyperparameters
alpha = 0.1
gamma = 0.99
epsilon = 0.1


# Training the agent
for episode in range(5000):
    state = env.reset()
```

```python
    state = tuple(state)

    if state not in Q:
        Q[state] = [0, 0, 0]  # Initialize Q-values for the state

    done = False

    while not done:
        # Epsilon-greedy policy
        if np.random.rand() < epsilon:
            action = env.action_space.sample()  # Explore
        else:
            action = np.argmax(Q[state])  # Exploit

        next_state, reward, done, _ = env.step(action)
        next_state = tuple(next_state)

        if next_state not in Q:
            Q[next_state] = [0, 0, 0]  # Initialize Q-values for the next state

        # Update Q-value using the Q-learning update rule
        Q[state][action] += alpha * (reward + gamma * max(Q[next_state]) -
Q[state][action])

        state = next_state
```

```
# Evaluate the trained agent
total_reward = 0
state = env.reset()
done = False

while not done:
    env.render()
    action = np.argmax(Q[tuple(state)])
    state, reward, done, _ = env.step(action)
    total_reward += reward

print("Total Reward:", total_reward)

env.close()
```

Exercise 3: Lunar Lander Game

```
import gym
import numpy as np

# Create LunarLander environment
env = gym.make('LunarLander-v2')

# Initialize Q-table
Q = {}
```

```python
# Hyperparameters
alpha = 0.1
gamma = 0.99
epsilon = 0.1

# Training the agent
for episode in range(5000):
    state = env.reset()
    state = tuple(state)

    if state not in Q:
        Q[state] = [0, 0, 0, 0]  # Initialize Q-values for the state

    done = False

    while not done:
        # Epsilon-greedy policy
        if np.random.rand() < epsilon:
            action = env.action_space.sample()  # Explore
        else:
            action = np.argmax(Q[state])  # Exploit

        next_state, reward, done, _ = env.step(action)
        next_state = tuple(next_state)
```

```python
    if next_state not in Q:
        Q[next_state] = [0, 0, 0, 0]  # Initialize Q-values for the next state


        # Update Q-value using the Q-learning update rule
        Q[state][action] += alpha * (reward + gamma * max(Q[next_state]) -
Q[state][action])


        state = next_state

# Evaluate the trained agent
total_reward = 0
state = env.reset()
done = False

while not done:
    env.render()
    action = np.argmax(Q[tuple(state)])
    state, reward, done, _ = env.step(action)
    total_reward += reward

print("Total Reward:", total_reward)

env.close()
```

Exercise 4: Deep Q-Network (DQN)

```python
import gym
import numpy as np
from tensorflow.keras.models import Sequential
from tensorflow.keras.layers import Dense
from tensorflow.keras.optimizers import Adam
from collections import deque
import random


class DQNAgent:
    def __init__(self, state_size, action_size):
        self.state_size = state_size
        self.action_size = action_size
        self.memory = deque(maxlen=2000)
        self.gamma = 0.95  # Discount factor
        self.epsilon = 1.0  # Exploration rate
        self.epsilon_decay = 0.995
        self.epsilon_min = 0.01
        self.learning_rate = 0.001
        self.model = self.build_model()

    def build_model(self):
        model = Sequential()
        model.add(Dense(24, input_dim=self.state_size, activation='relu'))
        model.add(Dense(24, activation='relu'))
```

```python
        model.add(Dense(self.action_size, activation='linear'))
        model.compile(loss='mse', optimizer=Adam(lr=self.learning_rate))
        return model

    def remember(self, state, action, reward, next_state, done):
        self.memory.append((state, action, reward, next_state, done))


    def act(self, state):
        if np.random.rand() <= self.epsilon:
            return random.randrange(self.action_size)  # Explore
        q_values = self.model.predict(state)
        return np.argmax(q_values[0])  # Exploit


    def replay(self, batch_size):
        minibatch = random.sample(self.memory, batch_size)
        for state, action, reward, next_state, done in minibatch:
            target = reward
            if not done:
                target = (reward + self.gamma *
np.amax(self.model.predict(next_state)[0]))
            target_f = self.model.predict(state)
            target_f[0][action] = target
            self.model.fit(state, target_f, epochs=1, verbose=0)
        if self.epsilon > self.epsilon_min:
            self.epsilon *= self.epsilon_decay
```

```python
# Create Deep Q-Network agent
env = gym.make('CartPole-v1')
state_size = env.observation_space.shape[0]
action_size = env.action_space.n
agent = DQNAgent(state_size, action_size)

# Training the agent
batch_size = 32
num_episodes = 1000

for episode in range(num_episodes):
    state = env.reset()
    state = np.reshape(state, [1, state_size])
    total_reward = 0

    for time in range(500):  # Maximum of 500 time steps per episode
        env.render()

        action = agent.act(state)
        next_state, reward, done, _ = env.step(action)
        next_state = np.reshape(next_state, [1, state_size])

        agent.remember(state, action, reward, next_state, done)
        state = next_state
```

```
        total_reward += reward

    if done:

        print("Episode: {}, Total Reward: {}, Epsilon:
{:.2}".format(episode + 1, total_reward, agent.epsilon))

        break

    if len(agent.memory) > batch_size:

        agent.replay(batch_size)

env.close()
```

Note: Ensure you have the necessary libraries installed (**gym**, **numpy**, **tensorflow**, **matplotlib**). Also, these are basic implementations, and depending on your requirements, you may need to adjust and enhance the code.

www.ingramcontent.com/pod-product-compliance
Lightning Source LLC
Chambersburg PA
CBHW070410290526
45791CB00005B/1698